# KITES

# KITES
## Sculpting the Sky
### BY TSUTOMU HIROI

Pantheon Books, New York

BOOK DESIGN BY KENNETH MIYAMOTO
assisted by Sara Eisenman and Gayle Waite

All rights reserved under International and Pan-American Copyright Conventions. Published in the United States by Pantheon Books, a division of Random House, Inc., New York, and simultaneously in Canada by Random House of Canada Limited, Toronto. Originally published in Japan as 凧—空の造形 by Bijutsu Shuppan-Sha, Tokyo, Japan. Copyright © 1972, 1975 by Tsutomu Hiroi.

*Library of Congress Cataloging in Publication Data*

Hiroi, Tsutomu, 1925–
Kites: Sculpting the Sky.

Translation of *Tako : sora no zokei.*
Bibliography: p. 146
Includes index.
   1. Kites.
TL759.H5613   629.133′32   76–62713
ISBN 0–394–73313–4 pbk.

Photographs on pages 10, 31–41, 44, 105, 120, 121, and 129 Copyright © by Akihisa Masuda.

Other photographs by Yoshiuki Sakai and Tsutomu Hiroi.

Manufactured in the United States of America
First American Edition

## ABOUT THE AUTHOR

Tsutomu Hiroi was born in Tokyo in 1925. Well known in Japan both as a sculptor and a kite designer, he is currently a professor at Tokyo Gakugei University. He is the author of six previously published Japanese books on kite-flying and kite design. He designed the Tokyo Kite Museum at Nihonbashi Taimeiken, which opened in 1977.

The author can be reached at 4–32–7 Kitakarasuyama Setagaya-ku, Tokyo 157 Japan.

# Foreword

If you have ever had a kite tug at your hand or your heart, you are on your way to Japan. You may not know it yet, but your journey is inevitable. Even if you don't get there in person, you will have made plans and built kites with the idea of going there someday. You will then travel not to Fuji or Kyoto or the regular tourist spots, but to those meccas of kite mystery and history—Shirone, Zama, Sagamihara, Hoshubana, Naruto, Hamamatsu—names associated with kites to match those of your dreams.

Then there are the byways, villages, and towns where, in tiny studios, master kite makers construct rare designs as patiently as if each kite were their first (and for someone it might be). These artists are carrying on centuries-old traditions yet simultaneously reinforcing their individual identities through kites that, long after the craftsmen are gone, will live in the skies—and in this book.

Every country that has its own kites should have its own Professor Hiroi. Although he is not the first to have written about the kites of Japan—and will not be the last—Hiroi is himself Japanese, a kite maker, an artist, and obviously a student of the kite culture of his homeland. His authority comes from knowing a subject from the inside out—as if it were a raincoat that he turns into a kite and back again. Simple?

Kites provide a good lesson about the essence of Japan. Such subtlety of craft makes kite flying appear effortless, and such control of design gives the maximum effect in the sky. And the kites are more varied than you can count—or than even Professor Hiroi can catalog. He tries, though, and it is his effort to bring order to this multifarious subject which we appreciate. What and where are the kites of Japan? How are they flown, and when? We know more answers to these questions now.

Furthermore, we learn of Hiroi's own deepest kite secrets, carried till now in his head and hands. They were previously locked in a book that was printed in Japanese. It is a tribute to Hiroi that on the strength of the photographs alone the Japanese edition has been collected by English-speaking kite buffs throughout the United States. At last these would-be readers' frustrations will be lifted with the publication of Hiroi's text in English. And the pictures, still there, prove again that kites are above all to be *seen*.

I predict that from this book forward, America's skies will never be the same. Not only has Hiroi set forth in usable form his own innovative, fresh, and very contemporary kite plans, he has presented general guidelines and instructions that apply to making all kinds of kites. Finally, he sets a standard for the dilletantes and dabblers among us when he dedicates his book to encouraging not only mere "technical perfection" but "ever more original creations." He does this in the best way possible—by example. Here is a reference book and then some, a source that is also a point of departure. Reading Hiroi's book offers almost enough inspiration to substitute for a trip to Japan. Next year, though, look for me at Hamamatsu!

—VALERIE GOVIG
Editor, *Kite Lines*
December 1977

# Acknowledgments

I would like to acknowledge the assistance I received from students at Tokyo Gakugei University and Tokyo Zokei University in assembling the material presented on three-dimensional kites in this volume. Thanks are also due to Makio Yamada, Yumiko Kato, and Etsuko Murakoshi for editorial assistance; to photographers Akihisa Masuda and Bijutsu Shuppan-Sha's Hiroyuki Sakai, who were most ardent in their kite photography even at the height of summer; and finally to my editor, Yoko Kono.

# Contents

# Preface

There is something miraculous about a kite. Earthbound, it seems to be merely another inanimate object, devoid of motion and life. Let it catch the wind, however, and it is transformed into a wondrous living creature. Watch as it dances its way up to the heavens and then pursues a zigzag course across the skies. Airborne, its shape and color merge in splendid harmony, while the kaleidoscopically shifting skies provide a spectacular backdrop. In the next instant, it has become one with the sky, and we wonder whether that exquisite, brief moment of beauty ever really existed.

It is this same fleeting encounter with beauty that brings the kite-flyer an almost sensual pleasure and a feeling of joy. There exists an empathy between the kite, as an extension of ourselves, and eternal, boundless nature. Through an upraised hand holding a single length of string, we experience the joining of heaven and earth.

Kiting has been called the celestial art. To appreciate the aptness of the term, it is enough to see a kite climbing gracefully to the sky, reflecting the glitter of the sun's rays, its shape changing with every gust of wind. If sculpture may be defined as "the art of systematically harmonizing and humanizing space," then the kite is surely a most promising form of modern sculpture. Artists have transformed the perception of space by expanding possibilities, introducing novel objects into space where they find a new freedom from gravity. Every aspect of kiting—from the colors, design, shapes, and materials used in their construction, to the very air, light, and movement in and by which they function—finds a counterpart in one of the innovations of the contemporary fine arts.

Perhaps even more significantly, flying a kite allows us to vicariously experience the incomparable joy of soaring freely through space, for flying is one expression of the desire of all life to reach new heights, the urge to grow. It is an expansion of freedom.

The kite as we know it today—in its many forms and variations around the world—is but the latest manifestation of a tradition reaching back twenty-five centuries to ancient China. From these early origins on, history is filled with the record of kites used as instruments in war, devices for signaling, exchanging information, and measuring, and as symbols of group solidarity and strength. In the West, the kite took on a new range of functions as a tool of scientific inquiry. Yet despite these demonstrations of the kite's versatility, most enthusiasts have abandoned utilitarian quests and enjoy the kite as it was originally conceived, as a glorious aesthetic and sporting pastime. Therefore, we should not forget the kite's primary purpose: to fly, and to fly well. In design and construction, the main objective is its proper functioning, toward which end we must direct all our creative resources. Every stage of the building process, from the fundamental calculations of weight, wing spread, and load, to the successful launching of the finished product, demands our utmost attention. Only then can we successfully combine inspired creativity and prosaic functionality to construct a well-flying kite.

After a brief survey of kiting history, we will move on to the careful construction of the basic box kite, discussing materials, design, and execution. From there, with experience and thought, you can conceive and develop kites of your own inspiration. For our concern goes beyond mere technical perfection to the production of ever more original creations.

*Hata* or fighting kite, dancing across the sky

# 1
# A Brief Look at Kites Through the Ages

Modern version of the primitive leaf-kite

Kite-making today is essentially the same as it was in its earliest beginnings. It consists of taking an object, attaching a string to it, and flying it through the air with only the wind as a source of power. And yet, throughout history, the fascinating diversity of design, function, and materials has made the kite a unique artifact of its time and place.

Credit for the first kite often goes either to ancient Chinese peasants, who tied strings to their hats, or to hunters, who adapted the idea from their practice of shooting arrows with string or rope attached. According to another theory, it was invented by natives of southern Indonesia, who flew tropical leaf-kites controlled by two pieces of string. This simple design was also known to peoples throughout Polynesia, the Solomons, and other Pacific islands. As suggested by the accompanying photograph, it is easily reproduced even today by connecting two theca leaves lengthwise with thin slats of bamboo. Other large tropical leaves, those of the banana for example, were also used, and suitable cords were available from the slender, sturdy vines native to these southern lands.

Historians tell us that in ancient Taiwan, the Ami people used the leaves of the bread-fruit tree to construct kites. Given the pro-pensity of the people of those times to believe in the spirits of the dead residing in a variety of unfamiliar objects, it is easy to understand how the astonishing sight of a kite soaring in the sky could inspire them to worship kites as religious symbols. In China and Taiwan, kites made of thin strips of bamboo plaited like flat baskets, with fishing lines attached to their tails, were used to catch fish.

Kites made of wood and cloth are known to have existed as early as two thousand years ago. The earliest surviving Chinese source, on kites, the *Han Fei Tzu*, describes the existence of the wooden kite during the third century B.C. There we are told that the philosopher Mo-Tzu, after three years of trial and tribulation, at last saw his kite airborne. Another work, the *Lu Wen*, tells the story of Mo-Tzu's disciple, Kung Shu Tzu, who succeeded in keeping a bird-shaped wooden kite aloft for as long as three days. Other records attest to the kite's usefulness from its earliest days as a surveying instrument in war. In 196 B.C., Han Hsin, statesman and general in the court of the Han dynasty emperor, is said to have used a kite to measure the distance to his enemy's fortifications, and with this information he was able to dig a tunnel and invade the enemy camp. This favorite Chinese tale has become the most widely embraced explanation for the invention of the utilitarian kite.

The advent of paper kites, however, came at a much later date, as the invention of paper in China is dated at 105 A.D. Thus, while we can only estimate the exact date of the first appearance of the kite, there can be no doubt of the vital role it played as man's messenger to the far-flung heavens, the focus of his most far-reaching dreams from the time of his own appearance on earth.

During the sixth and eighth centuries, the kite was widely used as a military signaling device. In 549 A.D., for example, during the Hou Ching Rebellion, a paper kite flown from a besieged castle signaled for reinforcements. The unobstructed visibility afforded by a high-flying kite made it possible to send and receive even complicated messages for miles around. Before long, the kite had replaced the rocket as a means of signaling troop positions.

It was only in the period of the Northern Sung (960–1126), the late Heian Period in Japan, that kite-flying became a popular pastime in China, its birthplace. However, it did not take long for kites to spread from China to neighboring lands, including India, Malaysia, and Polynesia, where they underwent distinctive courses of development in form and function.

In Korea, where kites arrived from China about 1000 A.D., rectangular kites similar to the prevalent Japanese form developed. It is still the custom, every year on January 15, to attach a fuse cord to the tail of a kite on which the words WARD OFF MISFORTUNE have been painted; the kite ignites in mid-air and flies off, taking with it, the fliers hope, all of man's ills.

The oldest known instance of kite-flying in Europe dates back to 230 B.C., when the Greek physicist Archimedes designed and flew a kite on which he had painted the portrait of the philosopher Plato. In the fourteenth century, kite-flying on horseback was in vogue among the German military. Subsequently, the bow kite, which became the most characteristic European kite, was developed in Germany; from there it made its way to France and England, where it was often used to set off fireworks in mid-air.

The popularity of kite-flying among the common people in the eighteenth century is reflected in Goya's painting depicting five men

"La Cometa," by Goya, 1778

flying a kite. One man holds a reel for winding the string; interestingly, the kite in the picture, consisting of a square shape turned on its end to look like a diamond in flight, is identical to the Nagasaki *hata* kite in every respect except for its European tail.

In 1749 two English astronomers, Alexander Wilson and Thomas Melville, attached a thermometer to a kite and were thus able to measure air temperature in the upper atmosphere. This is the earliest record of kites as instruments in scientific experiments. They proved to be more suitable for observation of meteorological phenomena at high altitudes than balloons under adverse wind conditions. In the nineteenth century, load- and line-bearing kites were employed in lifesaving and marine rescues.

Modern America boasts the invention of numerous excellent, aerodynamically refined kites. Yet, according to Stewart Culin in his *North American Indian Pastimes*, the kite did not exist in North America until the coming of the white man. Perhaps the most famous American kite story relates Benjamin Franklin's use of a kite to show that lightning discharges atmospheric electricity. In June 1756, when most people still fearfully regarded thunder and lightning as awesome manifesta-

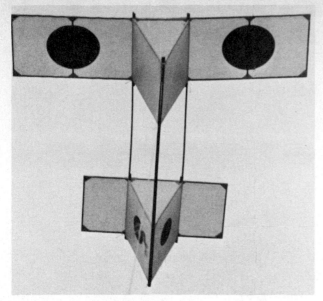

A modern airplane kite

Parasail, designed by Takehiko Sato

tions of God's wrath, Franklin used a kite to fly his testing rod higher than the tallest building. A small kite led him to invent the lightning rod and thus paved the way for the scientific study of electricity.

Of course, one of the kite's most important contributions to science has been in the study of flight in the development of the airplane. In an essay on "aerial navigation" published in 1809, England's Sir George Cayley outlined one of the fundamental principles of aeronautics when he explained that wind pressure on the inclined surface of a kite enabled it to lift weight. Cayley subsequently elaborated this principle and, in 1818, produced the first model glider, which actually had small kites for wings. He later was responsible for the first recorded manned glider flight. And, almost a century later, the Wright brothers also used kites to study the creation of airfoils and other wind dynamics in their attempt to master the control of lifting surfaces.

In the late 1920s, as people began to find it not quite so unusual to have machines flying above their heads, the "airplane" kite made its appearance. Essentially a three-dimensional kite, this creation features a V-shaped vertical section corresponding to the body of an airplane, and two flat, rectangular cross-sections, one long and one short, which function as

lateral and tail wings, respectively. When properly balanced and favored by a strong wind, this type of kite can reduce its angle of attack substantially and zoom upward as if oblivious to the wind's presence.

While the refinement of the airplane has obviously diminished interest in kites as serious vehicles of air transport, kites have recently enjoyed a whole new popularity in active sports such as water-skiing, where the water-skier is outfitted with a giant kite on his back. Towed by a motorboat, he will leave the water at a speed of about 25 miles per hour and ascend to a height of about 150 feet. When he wants to come down, he must signal the boat by waving his skis. It is up to him to achieve the difficult smooth, upright landing.

Yet another new dimension has been added to kite-flying as a sport by the parasail. These high-soaring kites are constructed with special attention to lifting power and direction control.

Another aeronautic sport, hang-gliding uses the delta wing kite. The rider glides down a sloping sand dune or a cliff, manipulating his body weight to keep the kite steady. Delta wing kites generally weigh about 20kg and have a variety of keel lengths, depending on the weight of the rider.

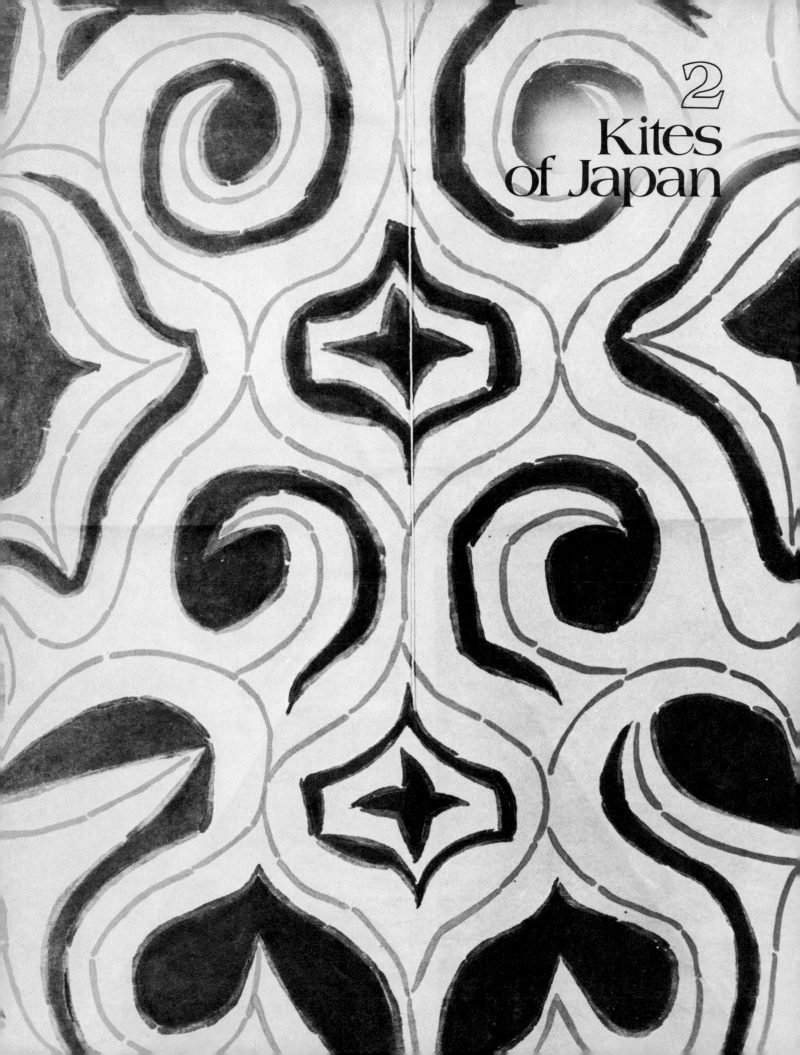

Kite-flying in the Heian Period, as seen in the Kyoto Festival

# An Ancient Tradition

Today, kiting takes on perhaps its most dynamic and dramatic form in Japan, where it has been a fully integrated part of the national heritage for over a thousand years. Some of the earliest Japanese documents extant, *The Chronicles of Japan* (720) and the *Hizen Almanac* (713), mention the existence of kites in the country. Records from the Heian Period (794–1185) assure us that wherever the first appearance of kites may have been in Japan, by that time people considered imported Chinese kites to be technically superior to anything existing on the local scene. Indeed, Japanese in the tenth century used a Chinese term meaning "paper hawk" to describe kites, which gives us further evidence that kites were of Chinese inspiration.

Present-day reconstitutions such as this depiction of ancient life at the Period Festival of Kyoto offer a glimpse of the way in which kites were flown during the Heian Period. In this sequence, a child skips rope as the two figures on the right fly a kite decorated with the ideograph for hawk.

As we have seen in other countries, there is evidence that kites were also being used in Heian Japan as a means of communication. The story goes that during the Later Three Year Campaign (1086–88), Shiro Ototashi, a retainer of Iehira Kiyowara, was able to establish contact with a moat-protected castle by attaching a secret message to a kite.

It was in the Edo, or Tokugawa, Period (1603–1868) that Japanese kiting attained maturity, growing from an aristocratic diversion—only the nobility and samurai could afford the high cost of paper—to a popular pastime. This development was made possible by technical advances in the art of woodblock printing, which facilitated the transformation of numerous *ukiyo-e* paintings into brilliantly colored *nishiki-e* (literally, "brocade pictures"), color print kites, adding a new level of refinement to the kite's evolution. Thus, even in these very early appearances, the distinctive Japanese talent for design manifested itself in the art of kite painting and decoration, where the pursuit of graphic excellence was paramount, as it remains today. Later development of calligraphic techniques made possible the fabrication of even more dramatic pictorial representations on kites.

Kiting gained further popularity with the emergence of a new and stable social order following the Warring States Period (1477–1573), which had been a time of brutal struggle among rival power groups. In the seventeenth century, the new stability under the Tokugawa gave rise to an ascendant merchant class. With them kiting was a popular activity, widely associated with the peaceful years following a century of war and turbulence.

Japan in its Edo Period could already claim an indigenous box-shaped, paper-lantern kite, perhaps the unacknowledged prototype of the modern three-dimensional kite. Also of long standing in Japan are cylindrical creations such as the fishlike *donko* and a variety of tubular warrior kites.

Today, there are some eighty-seven contemporary and historical kite centers throughout Japan, and the communal folk tradition of flying kites—particularly giant ones—has recently experienced a renaissance of noteworthy proportions. The Japanese have traditionally incorporated kites into their important religious, social, and political festivals and rituals. Many customs and celebrations which involve kites in present-day Japan originated centuries ago. It is recorded in the 1572 entry of the *Secret Records of Hamamatsu Castle* that "on the occasion of the Tango Festival on the fifth day of the fifth lunar month of the third year of Genki (1572), the vassal Tomomo Matsudaira and Hideyasu's retainers flew a diving beetle kite before the front gate." The mention of a distinct "diving bettle" (*gengoro*) kite here allows us to suppose that by this time there were already a number of different types of kites in existence. We also note here the association of kite-flying with the annual May 5 Boys' Festival, a day traditionally linked with the warrior class. It is from here that the contemporary custom of flying a kite to wish a newborn child health and happiness derives.

Another custom, involving the offering of celebrational kites (*iwaidako*) to one's lineal descendants, also derives from the Tango Festival. This custom expanded as kites became increasingly popular, and it became common for fathers as well as grandfathers to make kites for their descendants. They would draw likenesses of legendary heroes on the kites, which served as the bearers of their prayers for the worldly success of their progeny. This custom still exists today in such areas as Enshu Yokosuka and Boshu.

An even grander festival, and an outgrowth of the tradition, takes place today in Hamamatsu. There, upon the termination of the traditional kite-fighting competition, a kite float (*yatai*) circulates among all the homes where a male child has been born. Throughout Japan, parents continue to express their affection for children through the offering of warrior pictures or Kintaro baby warrior dolls, which symbolize courage and strength. The giant *oniyozu* demon kites of Mishima Island and the sleeve kites of Chonan are Tokugawa celebrational kites. A sleeve kite with a crane representation, which symbolizes longevity, might carry a strip of fancy paper on which was inscribed the name of the child being honored. Other celebrational kites might bear family crests.

Indicative of the eminence achieved by the kite among the common people of the Edo Period is the spectacular kite scene depicted by Hokusai in one of his famous "Thirty-six Views of Mount Fuji." This depiction of a distant snow-capped Mount Fuji framed by a high-flying rectangular kite and a *tombi* hawk kite fully captures the atmosphere of Edo Japan. The hawk kite pictured here, renowned among Edo citizens as the "hawk of

"View of the Mitsui Store in the Suruga District of Edo," from "Thirty-six Views of Mount Fuji," by Hokusai

Yotsuya," has retained its characteristic form to this day.

One interesting indication of the growing popularity of kiting was the number of kite edicts issued by the Shogunal government. For instance, an edict of January 6, 1656, stipulated that "kites shall not be flown by children in urban thoroughfares nor shall they be manufactured for commercial purposes." The exceedingly popular *nishiki-e* color print kites also exhibited an ostentation deemed improper by the authorities at this time. They fell victim to a rash of sumptuary regulations, and the vogue then shifted to the monochrome Yotsuya hawk kite, which, as both contemporary poetry and paintings attest, became almost a landmark of certain areas of Tokyo.

*Yotsuya of bamboo—*
*The coming of spring, bringing*
*Kite-flying and nightingales*

"Fukuroi in Shizuoka," from the Gyosho Tokaido series, by Hiroshige

"New Year's at Dawn," by Kuniteru Ichiyusai

Print by Hokusai from *Marvelous Tales of the Crescent Moon*, by Bakin Takizawa (1767–1848)

From Tokyo the kiting rage spread along the famous Tokaido highway to the rest of Japan. This print of Fukuroi in Shizuoka, from one of Hiroshige's Tokaido stage series, features a *buka* kite with a "sunrise crane" on it. The people on the ground are busy tying kite strings to trees or running with them—all in all, it is a scene overflowing with the joy of kite-flying.

Especially revealing of late-Edo kites is this *ukiyo-e* work, entitled "New Year's at Dawn." The large rectangular kite prominently featured here portrays actors performing in one of the popular "Soga Brothers' Revenge" plays (a twelfth-century tale of vengeance and filial piety) performed at New Year's around the turn of the eighteenth century. The women behind the kite are absorbed in a lively game of badminton, and in the background Kuniteru has presented a parade of different types of kites. From left to right: a sword kite; a *yakko* footman kite; a rectangular kite; a *tombi* hawk kite; an octopus kite; a dragon (ideograph) kite; and bringing up the rear, a five-kite *yakko* "train."

The kite fad of eighteenth-century Edo naturally found its way into the theater and popular storyteller repertoires. In December 1783 theatergoers at the Osaka Kakuza Theater viewed the first performance of a play based on the famous exploits of the thief Kinsuke Kakinoki, who, on February 14, 1712, took to the air aboard a giant kite and stole three scales from the golden dolphin of Nagoya Castle. His escape was unfortunately less successful, and the wily robber was eventually put to death in boiling oil.

Bakin Takizawa's *Marvelous Tales of the Crescent Moon* (1807–1811) tell how Tametomo Minamoto, exiled to Oshima Island following his defeat in the Hogen Rebellion (1156), tied his son to a kite and launched him in the direction of the mainland. Here we see the kite's safe arrival in Shimoda Bay. As the giant kite touches down, the samurai receiving the precious parcel sends up a smoke signal to inform the father that his son has arrived safely.

The existence of these tales testifies to the continuing fascination with kites through the ages. As for the veracity of these stories, one need only observe a kite in actual flight to find oneself nodding assent to their plausibility.

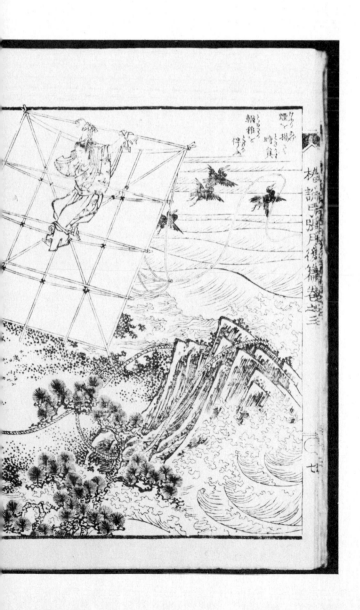

# Contemporary Styles and Designs

The word most commonly used to designate a kite in Japan today is *tako*, a homonym for the word for octopus. One early popular form of the kite was in fact an "octopus" kite. However, as the kite spread throughout Japan, each region developed its own distinct form and name, and these continue to be used by local residents.

Starting with the same indigenous materials—bamboo, paper, rope, and hemp line—skillful Japanese kite-makers miraculously created spectacular works of art from these elements. In the process, they fused a vigorous, living tradition with an infinite diversity of shape, construction, and elaborate design. The brilliant paintings that decorate the kites vividly express the local culture behind each kite as well as the spirit of the particular age in which it evolved.

Japanese kites generally can be divided into seven major categories, according to shape: rectangular; oblique; polygonal; round; intricate; windbag; and sleeve (or kimono). In addition to these shapes, there is a delightful variety of creative forms drawn from animals and insects, and a new style in children's kites.

Three broad types of kites also can be distinguished according to their geographic origins: the northern, which migrated directly from the Asian continent; the southern, which derived from the Southern Pacific; and the indigenous, which evolved solely within Japan.

The northern kites include some in the intricate category, such as the Goto Islands *bara-mon*, the Mishima Island *oniyozu*, and various kinds of *tojin* (foreigner or outsider) kites (p. 32, top). Because of their complexity of shape and design, these kites must have tails to retain their equilibrium in flight. Also of northern inspiration are the fan (p. 35, top), *yakko* footman (p. 21, top left), bee (p. 38), and *tombi* hawk (pp. 37, 38, bottom) kites, all of which feature a balloon-like windbag shape, considered to be a Japanese refinement of a less voluminous Chinese variety. When inflated, the curvature produced on the backside helps create lift.

The Nagasaki *hata* is the outstanding representative of the southern type. Its diamond shape, created by turning a square diagonally on end, appears to be a stylized abstraction inspired by the symmetry of the primitive leaf kite. The two bridles suspended from the vertical spine, combined with a flexible horizontal spar and rim, provide excellent stability. The *hata* can thus fly superbly without a tail, even in strong winds (p. 29).

The indigenous type features exceptionally beautiful rectangular and oblique-angle kites. The size of the rectangular kite varies according to its dimensions and the number of sheets of *nishinouchi* or uda paper used. The Japanese talent for skillful, efficient use of materials is especially evident in their thrifty use of just the right amount of paper.

## WINDBAG AND KIMONO SLEEVE KITES

The name of the *yakko*, a favorite kimono-shaped kite, comes from the word for footman or servant, traditionally the lowest class of person serving a warrior. The present-day custom in Usuki (Oita Prefecture) of flying *yakko* kites (p. 21, top) under a scorching August sun dates back to the time when the local lord, inspired by the Edo kite rage and oblivious to the time of year, ordered his subjects to take up kite-flying. Swordsmiths, who were in their slack summer season, were told to make kites. Having never wielded a paintbrush before, the ironworkers found themselves in something of a dilemma, which they resolved, as the story goes, by inventing the "backward-facing" complement of the original "front-facing" *yakko*; they simply painted their subjects from the rear point of view. These provided great amusement when the footman kite appeared to high-heel away—as the kite line was let out over the mansions of warrior lords.

The *yakko* kite was only one of many sleeve kites to make their way throughout Japan as the Edo kite craze spread. The waggish *sho-suke yakko* kite (p. 21, top right) from Osuga and the ingenuous *yokanbei* (p. 22) from Bungo Takada are undoubtedly variations of the *yakko*. Others, such as the *tenjin* (p. 21), *fukusuke* (pp. 22, 23), red kimono *daruma* (p. 21), and immensely popular contemporary children's *yakko* kites (p. 23, top right), make skillful use of the traditional *yakko*'s windbag technique.

The *sode*, or kimono sleeve kite (pp. 22, 23) is often given as a celebrational kite on the occasion of a newborn son's first Boys' Festival.

Edo *yakko* (Tokyo)

*Shosuke yakko* (Osua, Shizuoka Prefecture)

*Tenjin* (Anjo, Aichi Prefecture)

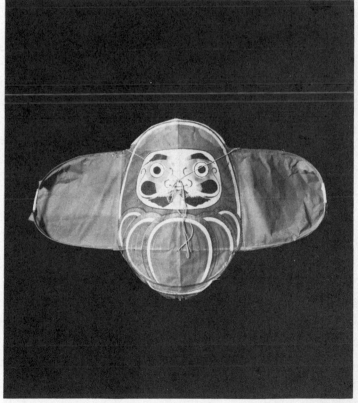

Windbag *daruma* (Tokyo)

Baseball star (Anjo, Aichi Prefecture)

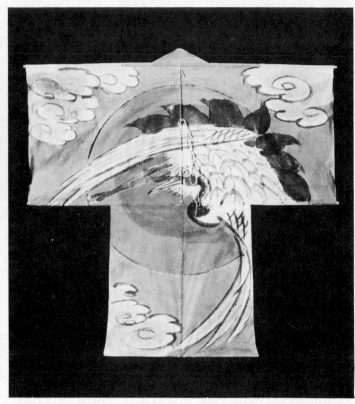

Sleeve kite with sunrise crane (Honno, Chiba Prefecture)

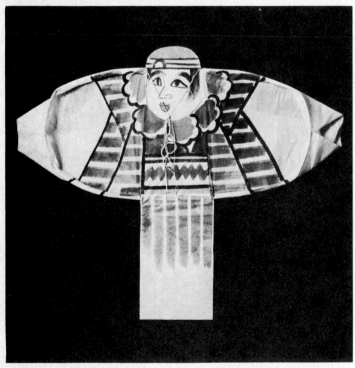

*Yokanbei* (Bungo Takada, Oita Prefecture)

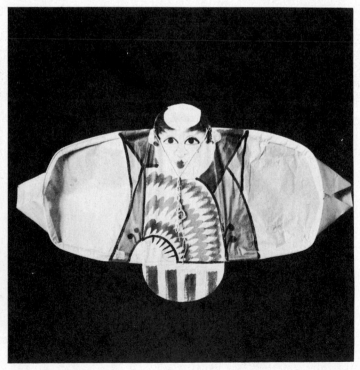

Saburo *fukusuke* (lucky gnome) (Bungo Takada, Oita Prefecture)

*Fukusuke* (lucky gnome) (Anjo, Aichi Prefecture)

Apollo spaceman (Tokushima, Tokushima Prefecture)

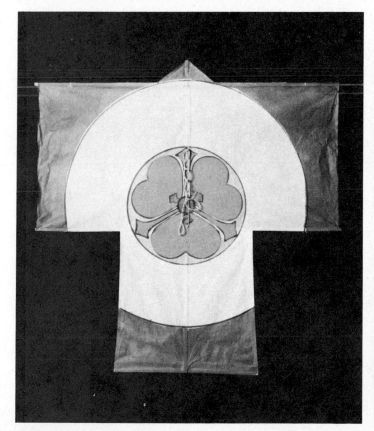

Sleeve kite with family crest (*jomon*) (Chonan, Chiba Prefecture)

Sleeve kite with golden carp (Chonan, Chiba Prefecture)

## RECTANGULAR KITES

The Edo *nishiki-e* (brocade picture) giant kite (pp. 24, 26), tailless and with a low wind speed, hums imperiously over the rows of houses below until it descends at nightfall. The tie point is set between the kite top and a distance one eighth of the way down. This allows the numerous other 36m-long bridle lines attached to the kite's bottom to lower the kite's center of gravity, stabilizing the kite as effectively as a rope tail. Special skill and experience are required to lower this kite safely in a strong wind. One must first draw in the flying line, then, holding onto the bridle base, pull just the bottommost bridle lines. This should cause the large kite to stand up perpendicularly and, in the next instant, meekly flutter down to the ground.

Commercially manufactured rectangular kites very often have bridles that are too short or bridle fittings that are too weak. Bridles should be at least two to three times longer than the kite.

Small rectangular kites should have their bridling points about one third of the way down from the top. They should also be bowed to allow for varying wind conditions.

*Managu* eye kites (p. 27) fly exceptionally well with their bridles aligned vertically.

*Hokkaido Ainu* kites (p. 27) have frames made of Japanese cypress rather than bamboo.

Dragon in clouds (Tokyo)

Dragon and jewels (*Nishiki-e* color print) (Tokyo)

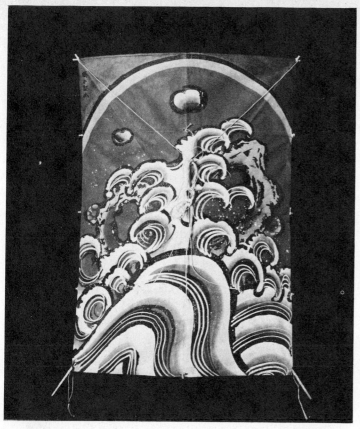

Rising wave (Tokyo)

*Daruma* (Tokyo)

Tsugaru (Hirosaki, Aomori Prefecture)

War epic (Yuzawa, Akita Prefecture)

Lion and peonies (*Nishiki-e* color print) (Tokyo)

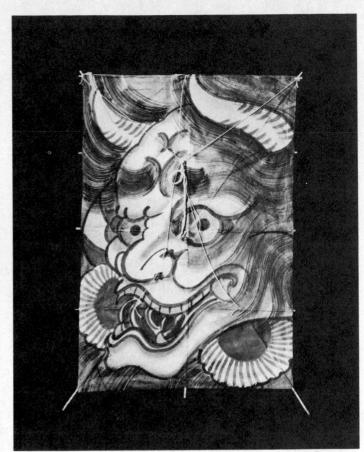

*Hannya* demon (Tokyo)

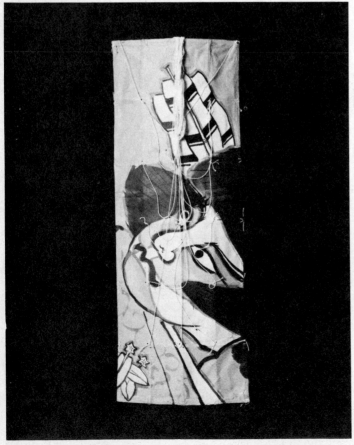

Tametomo Minamoto (long kite) (Hachijojima, Tokyo)

Devilish woman (Noshiro, Akita Prefecture)

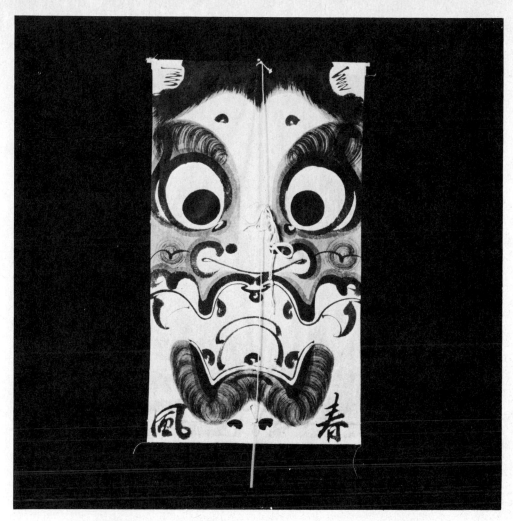

*Managu* eye (Yuzawa, Akita Prefecture)

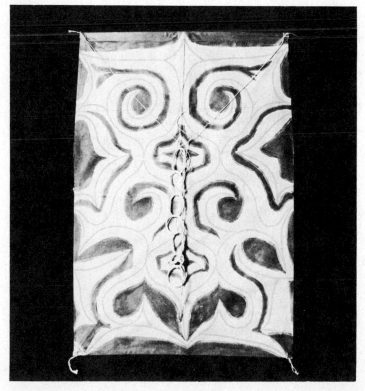

Ainu "Beneath Divine Eyes" (Hakodate, Hokkaido)

## OBLIQUE-ANGLE AND POLYGONAL KITES

The hexagonal *rokkaku* kite of Sanjo (Niigata Prefecture), nicknamed "squid" (*ika*), maintains good balance without a tail, provided the bridling is carefully done. Featuring a removable spine, which allows it to be rolled up like a tube, this kite is sometimes referred to as a tubular, or rolled, squid (*makiika*). The compact design is convenient both for transport and storage.

*Rokkaku* giant kites as long as 3.3m are used in the Shirone (Niigata Prefecture) competition. Graceful fliers, they require considerable strength to maneuver.

Takamatsu octagonal *hakkaku* kites (p. 31) may also be made collapsible.

And the *hikoichi* kite of Sawara (p. 31) flies efficiently with a single bridle line, thanks to the circular disk suspended from its lower front section.

*Rokkaku hexagonal* (Goro) (Sanjo and Shirone, Niigata Prefecture)

Kurayoshi (Kurayoshi, Tottori Prefecture)

*Ema* votive (Honno, Chiba Prefecture)

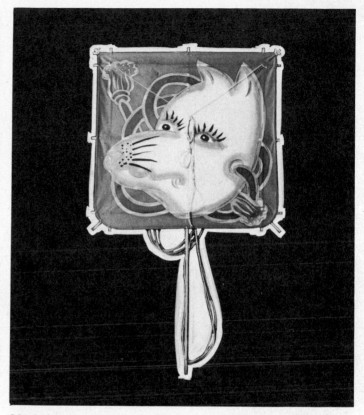

*Machijirushi* with fox (Hamamatsu, Shizuoka Prefecture)

*Hata* (Nagasaki, Nagasaki Prefecture)

*Mimimagari* (Chikujo and Bungo Takada, Fukuoka Prefecture)

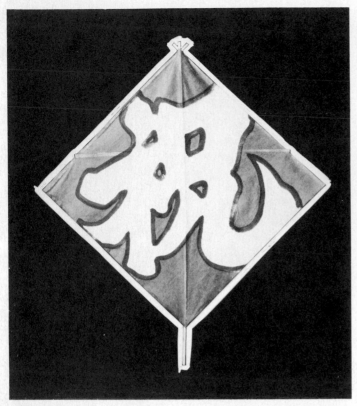

Tosa celebrational (Kagami, Kochi Prefecture)

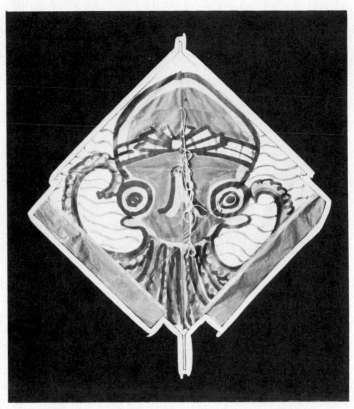

*Gonbo* squid or octopus (Takuma, Kagawa Prefecture)

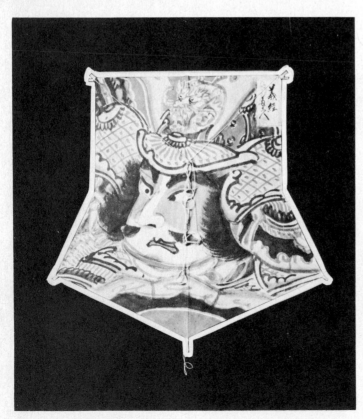

Suruga with Yoshitsune (Shizuoka, Shizuoka Prefecture)

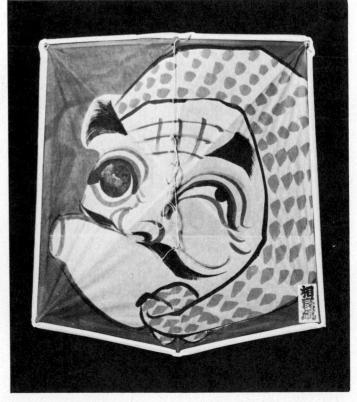

Sagara with *hyottoko* (droll fellow) (Sagara, Shizuoka Prefecture)

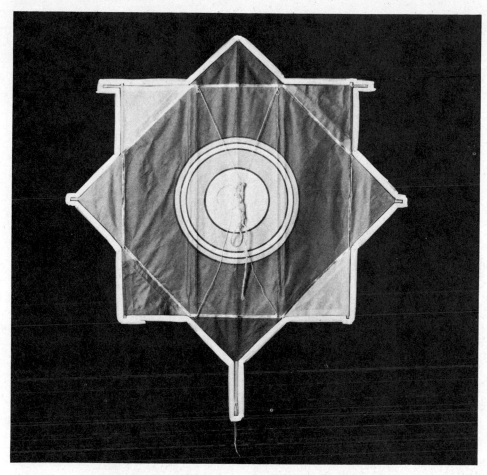

*Hakkaku* octagonal (Takamatsu, Kagawa Prefecture)

*Hikoichi* (Sawara, Chiba Prefecture)

## INTRICATE AND ROUND KITES

Especially popular among kites of Chinese origin, these intricately shaped kites are common in western Japan. The *oniyocho* is from Hirado (Nagasaki Prefecture) and the *baramon* is from Fukue in the Goto Islands. Most kites of this type feature complex and irregular contours, so they are usually fitted with thin bamboo strips around the edges to reinforce the shape. This tends to create a wind pressure differential, which usually makes a tail necessary.

Fan kites (p. 35) use the windbag form to advantage, while blowfish kites (p. 35) adapt the vent construction of Korean kites. Both fly superbly.

*Emmadojin* (King of Hades) (Koriyama Atami, Fukushima Prefecture)

*Oniyocho* demon (Hirado, Nagasaki Prefecture)

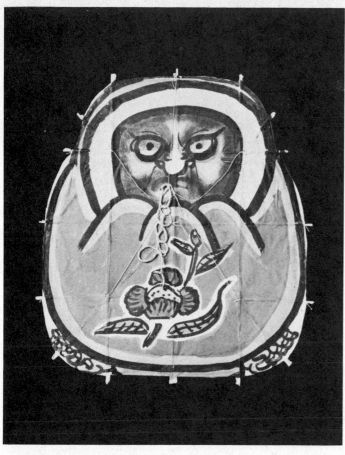

*Daruma* (Takumon, Kagawa Prefecture)

*Bekako* funny face (Osuka, Shizuoka Prefecture)

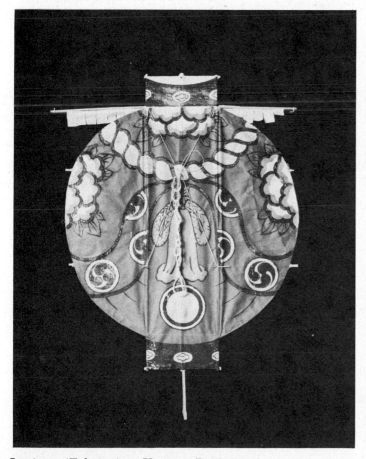

Lantern (Takamatsu, Kagawa Prefecture)

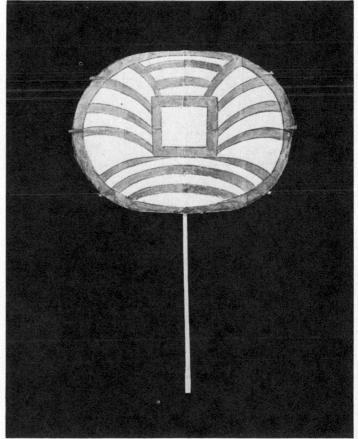

*Wan-wan* (Naruto, Tokushima Prefecture)

Orangutan (Takamatsu, Kagawa Prefecture)

Five-ring (Takamatsu, Kagawa Prefecture)

Izumo celebrational with crane ideograph (Taisha, Shimane Prefecture)

Izumo celebrational with tortoise ideograph (Taisha, Shimane Prefecture)

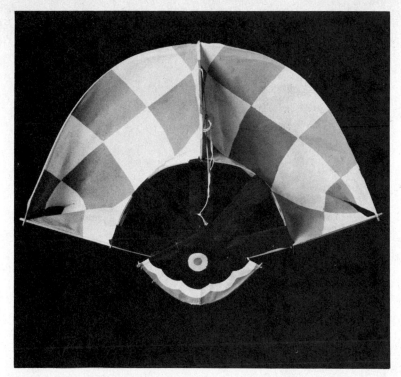

Fan (Anjo, Aichi Prefecture)

*Fugu* blowfish (Shimonoseki, Yamaguchi Prefecture)

## ANIMAL AND INSECT KITES

The *tombi* hawk kite (pp. 37, 38, bottom) has wings folded in such a way that a natural vented windbag results. On very windy days the bending backward of the wing allows air to enter. The size of the dihedral angle thus increases, improving overall stability. Accordingly, the *tombi* is a steady flier even in fairly strong winds.

The gadfly kite (p. 37) has a small red windbag around its curved body, making it an agile flier.

The body of the bat kite (p. 39) is triangular, three-dimensional, and collapsible.

Cicada (Takuma, Kagawa Prefecture)

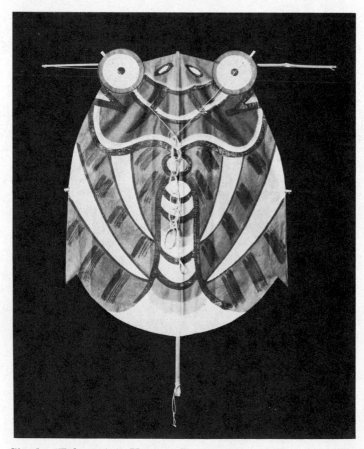

Cicada (Takamatsu, Kagawa Prefecture)

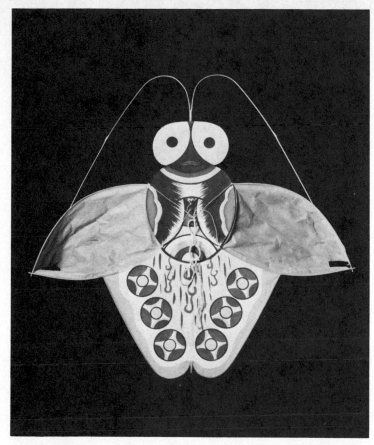

Butterfly (Anjo, Aichi Prefecture)

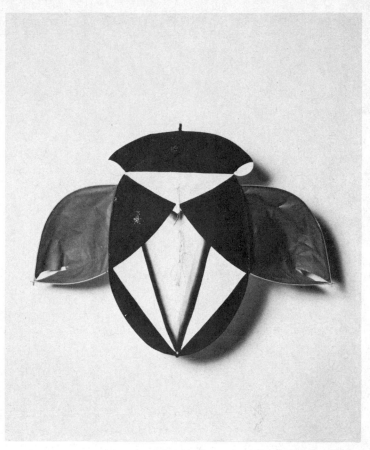

Gadfly, (Anjo, Aichi Prefecture)

*Tombi hawk* (Anjo, Aichi Prefecture)

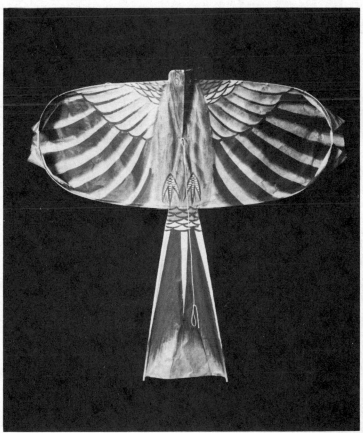

*Tombi* hawk (Osuga, Shizuoka Prefecture)

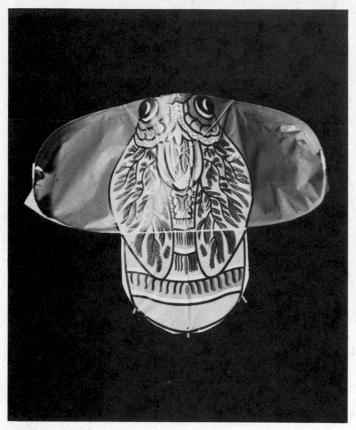

Cicada (Tokyo)

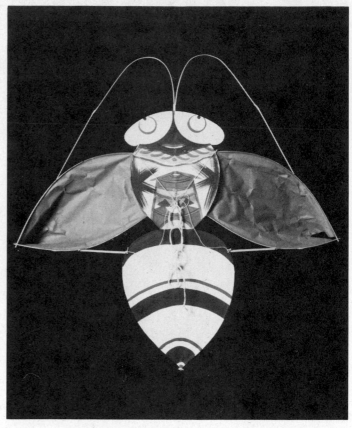

Bee (Anjo, Aichi Prefecture)

*Tombi* hawk (Tokyo)

*Tombi* hawk (Tokyo Region)

*Ikanobori* (squid banner) (Hakodate, Hokkaido)

Bat (Takamatsu, Kagawa Prefecture)

## CONTEMPORARY CHILDREN'S KITES

Children today seem to prefer kites featuring popular comic book or TV cartoon characters to the traditional demon (*hannya*) (p. 26) or *daruma* (p. 25) varieties. The occasionally seen "dragon" ideograph kite is probably more a reflection of adult nostalgia than anything else. In general, however, these kites reflect children's rapidly changing likes and dislikes as well as their heroes of the moment, and thus may be considered as a convenient barometer of the trends of our times. An indication of the harried and dangerous times we live in is the "traffic safety" kite (p. 43).

Spinning-top *koma* kites (p. 41, bottom; p. 43, top) were devised in the late nineteenth century by the head priest of Senju, and they instantly spread throughout Japan. Of very simple construction, and able to fly in a light breeze using any type of string, these kites are popular among children all over.

Rectangular with dragon ideograph (Tokyo)

Moon voyage (Tokyo)

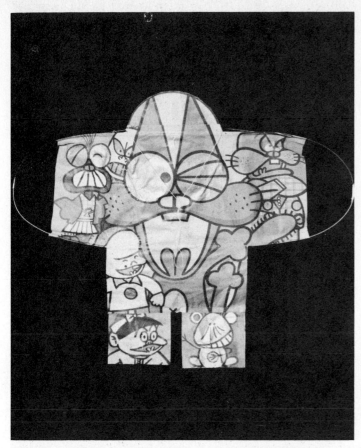

*Nyarome* (Tokushima, Tokushima Prefecture)

*Norakuro* (Tokyo)

*Gegege no Kitaro* (Tokyo)

Oba Q (Tokyo)

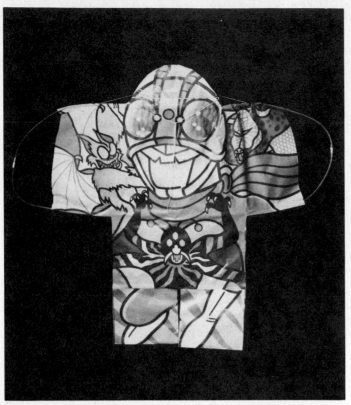

Masked rider (Tokushima, Tokushima Prefecture)     Spectrum man (Tokyo)

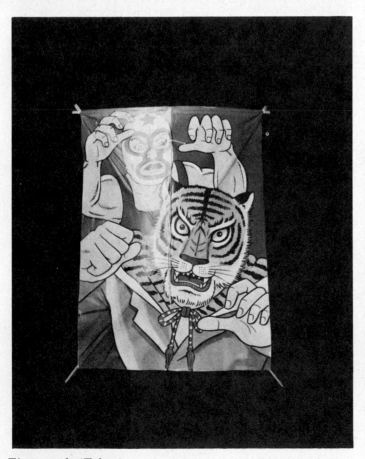

Tiger mask (Tokyo)     Rustic general (Tokyo)

Giant baseball star (Tokyo)

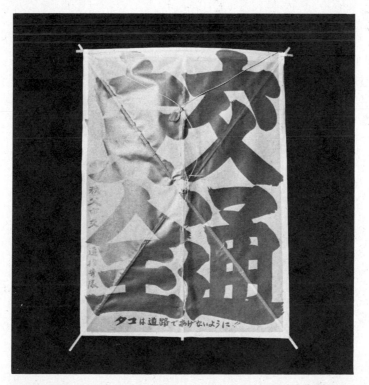

Rectangular with traffic safety ideograph (Chichibu
City, Saitama Prefecture)

*Oniyozu* demon kite

## ONIYOZU DEMON KITE

On the solitary island of Mishima in the Japan Sea, facing the city of Hagi (Yamaguchi Prefecture), kites are referred to by a special term, *yozu*, which, among its other connotations, suggests demonic force. Having sustained repeated invasions from Korea, islanders took to flying these terrifying demon kites both as a prayer for protection and as a warning to the enemy to keep away.

Today, when a first son is born, relatives and friends get together just before the New Year and fly this kite to express their hope that the child will take after the vigorous kite and grow to be robust and strong. The larger models, which are flown on the morning of New Year's day, may be as long as 16m on a side. The demonic face is painted red, blue, and black, colors said to have the power to ward off evil spirits.

# Japan's Giant Kites

Kites were improved considerably during the Edo Period as they passed from the hands of the nobility to the common people. The latter held kite-flying contests for kite enthusiasts throughout the country, and their children adopted the kite as a new toy. The elders meanwhile developed distinctly adult forms of kite recreation—fighting-kite and giant-kite competitions—which gradually assumed the nature of ritual fests and finally evolved into veritable folk traditions.

Kite battles featuring mammoth kites developed into traditional annual rivalries between neighboring communities. In this exciting ritual-sport, teams man highly maneuverable giant kites flown on lines glazed with powdered glass. They attempt to sever—and, if possible, capture—their opponents' kites through careful aeronautic tactics. Today, among the best-known annual kite events are those of Shirone and Sanjo (Niigata Prefecture), which take place in June, and Hojubana (Saitama Prefecture), Sagamihara, and Zama (Kanagawa Prefecture) in May. Attended by the entire populace, the festivities include day-long drinking and feasting as well as kite-flying. Probably the most spectacular giant kite battle is that held in Hamamatsu (Shizuoka Prefecture) every May 3–5. Nagasaki's *hata* kites are the prime combatants in the profusion of small fighting-kite events taking place from February through April 8.

The phenomenon of the giant kite, unknown outside Japan, may reflect a distinct Japanese predilection for group cohesiveness. Over the years, the kites of each festival have developed their own distinct size, shape, and features. The following list demonstrates once again the remarkable variety of kite skills, traditions, and forms represented in these festive celebrations.

Flying giant kites in Yokaichi City: "A Glorious and Prosperous National Destiny," 1902

Sagamihara giant kite, back view

Launching the Sagamihara giant kite, with "Up and Coming" ideograph

Shirone giant kite featuring Momotaro,
a popular children's story hero

Hojubana giant kit with "Tops in Japan" ideograph

Naruto giant *wan-wan* kitc

Sanjo *rokkaku* hexagonal giant kite

Hamamatsu Kite Festival: sixty-six kites
from sixty-six neighborhood districts

Launching the giant kite in Zama

Transporting the giant kite in Shirone

## Giant-Kite Festivals

### Sagamihara (Kanagawa Prefecture)

Date: May 6–7

Site: Sagamihara, at Shintogawara along the banks of the Sagami River

History: Flown by private individuals in the 1830s to celebrate the birth of a new-born son, giant-kite flying by the end of the nineteenth century had become associated with good harvests and nationalistic pride.

Features: Size: 12.6m square
Weight: about 1,000kg
Paper: 1,500 sheets (33cm × 48.5cm) of *washi* paper
Kite line: hemp (about 3cm thick)
Frame: durable

Flying: The flying of these mammoth kites, requiring at least one hundred people, is generally performed by the members of the Araiso Giant Kite Preservation Association, although non-members may also participate.

### Zama (Kanagawa Prefecture)

Date: May 6–7

Site: Zama, at Shintajuku along the banks of the Sagami River

History: Zama's giant kites, a tradition since the 1890s, are distinguished by their pithy inscriptions, e.g., "zephyr," "good omen."

Features: Size: 11m square
Weight: about 700kg
Paper: *washi*
Kite line: hemp

Flying: Members of the Zama City Youth Association assume the major part of the responsibility. Colorful floats add to the festive atmosphere along the river banks, where the kites are burnt on the last day of the festivities.

### Shirone (Niigata Prefecture)

Date: June Iris Festival

Site: Nakanokuchi River

History: Giant-kite fighting here is said to have originated three hundred years ago, when kites flown as part of a canal repairing celebration by the people of Shirone in Shibata County dropped on the west bank, causing damage to farmhouses and rice crops. In retaliation, the west Shirone farmers began flying kites themselves, giving rise to the present ongoing rivalry.

Features: Size: 7.25m × 5.45m
Weight: about 200kg
Shape: rectangular or hexagonal (3.33m)
Paper: 400 sheets of *nishinouchi* paper
Decoration: warrior paintings, etc.
Frame: durable

Flying: The two communities, located respectively on the eastern (Shirone City) and western (West Shirone) banks of the Nakanokuchi River do battle to bring down their rivals' kites. The fight is not over even after the downing of the kites, as final victory goes to the side that retrieves its kite from the river via a monumental tug of war.

## Hamamatsu (Shizuoka Prefecture)

Date: May 3–5
Site: Nakatajima Beach
History: Hamamatsu giant kiting goes back four hundred years to the Eiroku Era (1558–70). The target of numerous edicts banning kites from 1807 to the end of the Edo Period (1868), the sport underwent a large-scale revival in the late nineteenth and early twentieth centuries.

Features: Size: about 3.3m square
Weight: about 10kg
Paper: *mino* handmade paper
Kite line: Shinshu twisted flax
Decoration: painted letters, insignias, etc., designating the neighborhoods represented

Flying: At the sounding of a trumpet, a profusion of kite lines representing all of Hamamatsu's sixty-six neighborhood districts come to life and struggle valiantly to assert their dominance over this section of the sky. When it is all over, they are hauled in with the aid of a special pulley (*tegi*).

## Hojubana (Saitama Prefecture)

Date: May 3 (Constitution Day) and May 5 (Children's Day)

Site: The Edogawa River at west Hoshubana
History: Kites were introduced here in 1730 as a method of divination for the forthcoming year's silkworm crop. Originally smaller, the kites reached their present-day size in the late nineteenth century.

Features: Size: about 15m × 11m
Weight: about 800kg
Paper: 1,500 sheets of *nishinouchi* paper
Bridle legs: 200, each 35m long
Decoration: newborn children's names or prayers sometimes inscribed on the kite

Flying: Fifteen heavy rice bags are hooked up to the kite after launching to serve as an anchor. Launched in the late afternoon, the Hoshubana giant is usually flown for about an hour and lowered at sunset. The flyers, wearing headbands and white ceremonial *happi* coats with red and green insignias, heroically begin the launching at the chiming of an iron bell.

## Naruto (Tokushima Prefecture)

Date: June–July
Site: Hiroto Beach, Okazaki
History: In June 1692, on the occasion of the dedication ceremony celebrating the reconstruction of the Rengeji Temple in the Okazaki District of Naruto City, a circular kite made of fifty sheets of uda paper was flown by the construction foreman Mataemon. Giant kiting in Naruto was in vogue in the 1930s and is now undergoing a revival.

Features: Size: *wan-wan* kite—24m in diameter
*kikuichi* kite—22m in diameter
Shape: circular
Weight: about 2,500kg
Paper: as many as three thousand sheets of uda paper
Decoration: stylistic representation of names

Flying: The competing kites used to be ranked according to size. In 1935 there were 103 kites entered. A heavy "block" pulley system and sandbags would be used, along with the force of two hundred men, to bring these kites back to earth.

# 3
# The Fundamentals of Kite-making

# Basic Principles of Aerodynamics

Air—colorless and invisible to the naked eye. We, who live surrounded by it, are apt to overlook its existence, unless, by chance, we detect its presence in the rustling of the leaves of a nearby tree and call it wind, or if we are floating down to earth in an open parachute, happily taking maximum advantage of the air in our vicinity.

The density of air on the earth's surface (air pressure) fluctuates considerably, even at given altitudes, causing low and high air-pressure areas. The former signify places where the air pressure is lower than its surroundings, producing an influx of air from the immediate vicinity. In a high-pressure area, the flow of air is outward, the result of an air pressure higher than that of the surrounding area. It is this air flow which creates wind.

Wind velocity may be gauged through observation of natural phenomena (see wind velocity chart in the Appendix) or by using an anemometer, a compact, portable device that measures average wind speed in meters per 100 seconds.

Wind flow is influenced by conditions on the earth. In coastal areas the wind blows toward the land during the day but toward the sea at night. These phenomena are known as land and sea breezes. During the day, coastal areas absorb solar heat and become warm, causing the air there to heat, expand, and become lighter. This produces a low air-pressure zone, forcing wind to blow in from the sea. At night, the land mass rapidly cools off, resulting in a flow of wind from the land back toward the sea.

Anemometer, for measuring precise wind velocity

When wind strikes a steep mountain slope, an updraft is created. In places where this happens, you may see birds gliding in mid-air for long periods of time without even flapping their wings. On the opposite side of the mountain, meanwhile, an air eddy will form, resulting in a downward wind draft. These rapid airflows inevitably arise in the vicinity of trees, buildings, and other topographical irregularities. The diagram shows what happens when a wind flow encounters natural and man-made obstacles.

Everyone knows that objects have weight and that if they are released in mid-air, the force of gravity will immediately cause them to fall. It is perhaps less well understood that the reason a kite weighing as little as 5g or as much as 800kg can fly is that there is another force helping to support its weight. This upward directed force is known as lift.

When wind strikes the surface of a kite, the air bifurcates, or divides; part of it flows up and part down, creating an airfoil. The downward moving air is bent and hindered in its movement. As a result, its velocity drops, the air pressure beneath the kite rises, and the kite surface is thrust upward. Meanwhile, the upward moving air flows more easily, increasing its speed as its air pressure drops, thus pulling the kite upward. Lift may be considered the product of this differential in air pressure.

As lift acts to sustain the weight of the kite in the air, another crucial force works to push the kite downward. This is frictional resistance, which the air exerts against any object. Known as drag, it can be felt most acutely as a pull on the flying line.

The lift-to-drag ratio varies according to the position of the tie point. When it is relatively low, drag is increased, and a strong pull on the line will cause the kite to fly in a horizontal direction. When the tie point is located near the kite top, on the other hand, lift is increased, drag reduced, and the kite flies vertically, for in this case the pull on the line is weaker than that on the lower bridle leg.

Stability is determined by the kite's dimensions and the angle at which it is attached to its line. Stability varies in two coordinated directions: longitudinally and latitudinally, according to the lengthwise and crosswise axes of the kite itself.

To better understand how stability is determined, consider the airplane in horizontal flight. If the nose of the plane rises due to the wind, there will be a corresponding increase in the tail's angle of attack (the angle of the wing surface relative to the wind flow). This will increase the amount of lift operating on

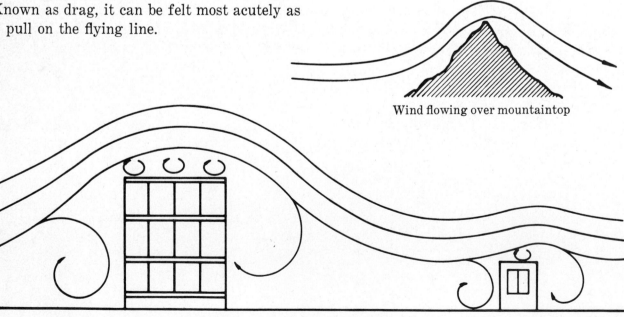

Wind flowing over mountaintop

Wind flowing over various sized buildings

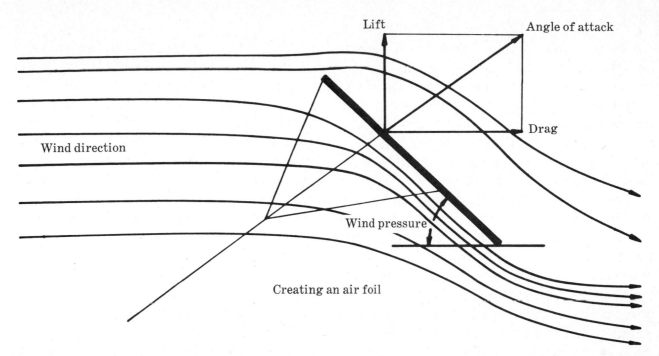

Lift

Angle of attack

Drag

Wind direction

Wind pressure

Creating an air foil

the tail, causing it to rise. This, in turn, will produce a rotating force known as moment, which pushes the nose downward toward the plane's center of gravity and sets into motion a longitudinal stabilizing effect that will restore the plane to its normal level position.

In kites, particularly three-dimensional ones, this ratio between the main wing and the tail wing is distorted. Certain kites cannot fly at all without a tail to restore longitudinal stability. Many others are perfectly good and steady fliers without this assistance. The *tombi* hawk kite, for example, whose wings and tail correspond to the lateral wings and tail of an airplane, can usually fly without a tail.

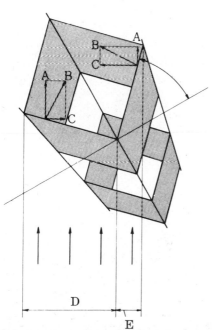

The above diagram illustrates the position of the dihedral angle in the box kite, together with the lift or vertical component force (A), actual lift (B), and horizontal component force (C). As the kite inclines, wing span D increases, while wing span E decreases.

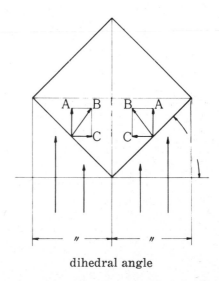

dihedral angle

In the above diagram, wing spans D and E are the same, as the kite's stability has been restored.

To maintain lateral stability, an airplane's wings are raised slightly so that the tips are higher than the center of the plane. This creates a "dihedral angle," which helps maintain equilibrium by preventing lateral rolling. If the airplane should begin to roll, or incline to one side, this dihedral angle will allow more air to reach the wing on that side, thus increasing its lift and restoring the aircraft to a horizontal position.

For kites, which must fly without the benefit of a pilot, an adequate dihedral angle as an automatic stabilizer is a must. The very design of three-dimensional kites incorporates the necessary angle in the relationship of the various surfaces of the structure. The majority of flat or two-dimensional kites can achieve the same end as three-dimensional ones by bowing or curving the surface—stretching a length of line from both ends of the horizontal spar. In high winds, increasing the arc of the bow will lend added stability to the kite.

A kite, like an airplane, can also deviate from its stable course in a third direction, around its vertical axis, a hazard known as yawing. A large dihedral angle (functioning in the same way as the perpendicular section of the tail of a plane) eliminates this problem.

To control the kite's angle relative to the wind, as a pilot would in an airplane, a line called the bridle (generally two-pronged) is attached to the kite at any of several points along the vertical spine. The legs or spokes then come together at the tie, or bridling, point, where they attach to the flying line. This will accurately set the kite's center of pressure and enable it to resist strong winds. The precise arrangement and adjustment for the individual type and size of kite will be included in the instructions for constructing and flying box kites (see pp. 69–78).

When you begin to design and construct your own variations of the box and other three-dimensional kites, take care to observe

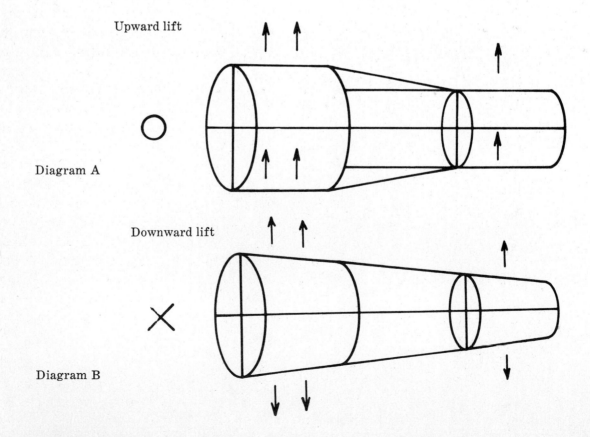

Upward lift

Diagram A

Downward lift

Diagram B

these basic aerodynamic principles, or you may find yourself with an intricately designed and constructed kite that simply will not fly. Take, for example, a three-dimensional kite with streamer-like tapered ends, as illustrated in the accompanying diagram. The same principle applies as in the case of biplanes. If the attack angles of the upper and lower wings face in opposite directions (Diagram A), the wing surface will produce upward lift while the lower one produces downward lift. They will thus cancel each other out, making flight impossible. Hence, three-dimensional kite faces should always be parallel to each other (Diagram B).

It is possible to make kites that will fly in an unusual manner. This can be done by inserting a pinwheel in a three-dimensional kite, or by constructing a wing surface which can change its own wind direction. The drumcan kite (p. 102) flies magnificently with its entire body rotating on a pinwheel mechanism.

In the following pages we shall design and construct several types of kites. We shall consider these instructions not as blueprints to be copied but as design targets to be approached. We shall seek to combine creativity with structural efficiency. And only after we have constructed what we have designed, then bowed and bridled it, will we experience the true exhilaration of kiting, which is to witness the creation of one's own ingenuity and skill soaring splendidly through the skies.

# Materials and Equipment
## CHOOSING A KITE LINE

Kite lines may be made of cotton, hemp, nylon, or various other materials, but the thickness and strength you select must be in proportion to the size and weight of your kite.

Kite string is actually made up of several individual strands of line twisted together in units of three. The number-labels for the line refer to the size and number of strands it contains. For example, a No. 20 count 10 line is composed of three 10-strand units of 20-count cotton thread. You can verify the thickness yourself by unraveling the piece of line and counting the strands.

One general rule to follow in choosing an appropriate line is to select a line with a test or breaking strength (in kilograms) that is fifteen times the kite's surface area (in square meters). Most commercial lines indicate the test strength of the particular size. A 180m length of No. 20 count 5 string weighing 100g has a breaking strength of 7kg, while a 90m length of No. 20 count 10, also weighing 100g, breaks at 13kg.

Hemp line (No. 16 count 4 or 5) is thinner but stronger than cotton. Nylon thread is the strongest, but it is also slippery and very thin, and must be handled directly from a reel. Nylon line comes in thicknesses of 3, 4, 5, 6, 9, and 12mm.

It is best to purchase the longest possible length, calculate the length you will need for a particular kite and flight, and wind it on a reel. If lines are not to become entangled, they must be carefully handled. The best guarantee of this is to use a kite reel. When attaching the line to the reel, make sure the end is securely fastened, or you may find your kite taking off on its own. Even cotton line may cut your hand if it is let out rapidly in a strong wind; so, in addition to the reel, gloves are advisable and caution mandatory. Always take care not to step on or otherwise damage your line.

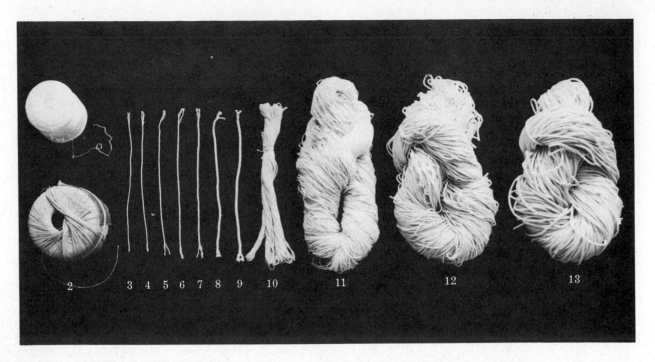

1. No. 40 count lace thread (about 1,000m) (top left)

2. No. 20 count 3 flax string (bottom left)

3. No. 20 count 3 cotton kite string (left to right)

4. No. 20 count 5 cotton kite string

5. No. 20 count 10 cotton kite string

6. No. 20 count 15 cotton kite string

7. No. 20 count 20 cotton kite string

8. No. 20 count 30 cotton kite string

9. No. 20 count 40 cotton kite string

10. No. 20 count 5 cotton kite string, 10g bundle

11. No. 20 count 5 cotton kite string, 150g bundle

12. No. 20 count 10 cotton kite string, 250g bundle

13. No. 20 count 25 cotton kite string, 400g bundle

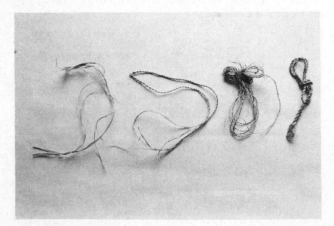

Kite string made by the children of remote Aoga-shima Island. Using the rose mallow native to the island's hot springs, their hands turn red from the plant pigment as they extract the fiber, producing the twine shown on the right in the photograph.

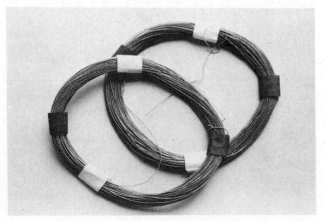

Glass-coated hemp line (*yoma*) for Nagasaki fighter kites. This dangerous flying line will be used to sever the lines of opponents' kites, and must be handled on a reel, so that it is not touched with bare hands.

# KITE KNOTS

Only a few basic knots are needed to construct most kites. The square knot is the most common. Cross the two ends, passing one under the other. Cross them a second time, forming a square or ring. Now pass one end through the opening and pull both ends tight.

To make a vertical, or granny, knot follow the procedure for the square knot, but when forming the square, cross the strings in the opposite direction so that when you tighten them, the ends are aligned vertically.

A whirl knot is formed by holding two lengths of line together, creating a circle. Pass the end of your double strand through the circle and tighten. It is best to leave an extra 1.5cm of line extending beyond the knot. This is a good knot for bunching the bridle lines.

A clove hitch is a knot used to bow rectangular kites. Hook the line into a loop, then into a double loop. Pull on the nearer end to tighten.

When tying the bridle to the kite frame, use a vertical knot, leaving a good 7–8cm extra,

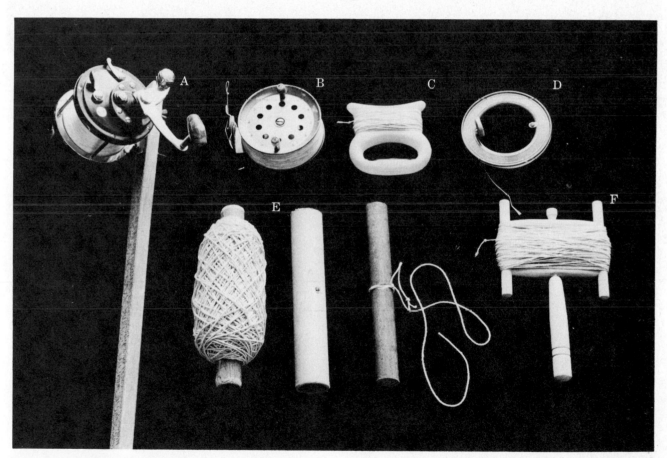

Kite reels. Fishing reels found in fishing-supply stores (A,B,D) make excellent kite-line reels. The easy-to-handle plastic reel (C) is recommended for children. You can also use a stick or cardboard tube (E); wind the line on in a figure-eight fashion with your right hand while holding the stick firmly with your left. The string-winding reel designed specifically for kite-flying (F) comes in a variety of shapes.

The large reel held here by Takeshi Nishibayashi, maker of the Korean kite described on page 121, features a 50cm-long stick attached to its center axle, which enables the flier to handle the kite without ever touching the line with his bare hands, an absolute necessity when using thin line or line coated with ground glass for fighting kites. Brace the stick under the arm when giving out line; to reel in, hold the stick in the right hand and rotate the filature with the left.

Bamboo baskets or other receptacles are convenient for transporting the line after it has been hauled in. Loosely woven baskets may be lined with *washi* paper before use.

This reel, used for the giant kites in the Hamamatsu festival, is anchored to a flatcar fully equipped with clutch and brakes.

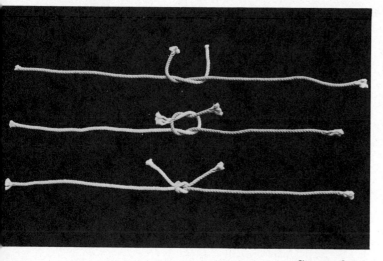

Square knot

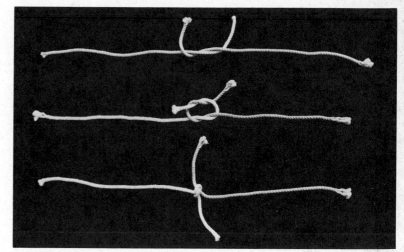

Vertical knot

which should then be attached to the bridle line with a simple knot (see photograph). For especially thick frames, use doubly thick line and attach it to the bridle with a vertical knot. To tie the bridle and the flying line, make a knot and a loop at the end of the flying line so that when you pull on the free end, it will come loose. Always test this section of line before launching to make sure it is securely fastened.

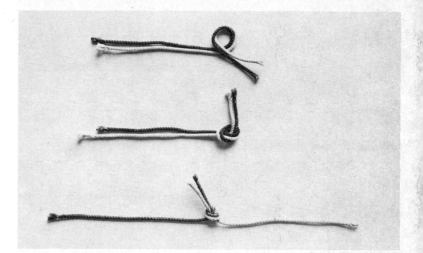

Whirl knot

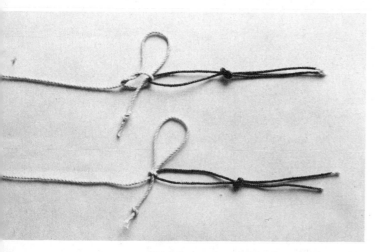

Attaching the bridle to the flying line

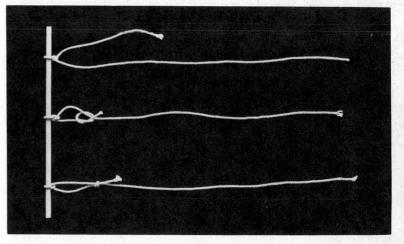

Attaching the bridle to the kite frame

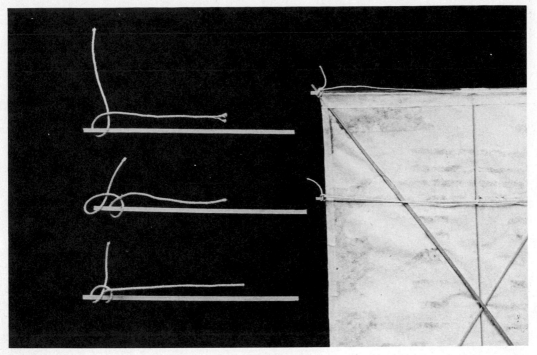

Clove hitch

## KITE PAPER AND DECORATING

Kite paper usually means Japanese handmade *washi* or its most common variety, *nishi-nouchi* paper. There are other kinds of high quality *washi* that are suitable for kites, however, such as that used for paper lanterns or umbrellas.

*Washi* is made from fibers extracted from *kozo* or *mitsumata* plants. Made by hand, its long fibers overlap vertically and horizontally to produce a light, soft, yet sturdy product.

Western paper is made from wood pulp and has relatively short, hard fibers; it tears easily and is therefore unsuitable for kites. Recently, tough synthetic fibers, cheaper and easier to procure than the handmade *washi*, have become popular among kite enthusiasts.

Traditional silk kites are still made today in China, where kites evolved long before the invention of paper. These are as strong and lightweight as ever, and do not tear even when wet. Japan also produced a variety of cloth kites during its Edo Period; and today cotton, nylon, and other light, fine-textured cloths are most often preferred for collapsible kites.

Kite and hobby shops now carry a variety of plastic materials which have different advantages and drawbacks. In the box kite we will build first, I use vinyl sheeting for wings. Lightweight, water-resistant, and transparent, it is ideal for box kites. Vinyl isn't perfect, however; it shrivels with time or in high temperatures and is easily ripped by sharp objects. Always make sure the vinyl is smooth when using it to construct kites. If the vinyl tears anyway, cellophane tape may be used for emergency repairs.

You may prefer to use polyethylene film (0.03); note the polyethylene bag used for the *gunya-gunya* kite.

In Japan, special regional adaptations have evolved in kite materials as well as in design, taking into account the environment in which a kite will be flown. For example, the *managu* eye kites of the Yuzawa region (Akita Prefecture), which are flown in the snow, are coated with persimmon tannin to make the paper especially water-resistant. In general, Japanese kite-makers favor the paper produced in their own region.

Color is usually achieved by the generous application of a mixture of colorant with very slight amounts of alum and glue. Transparent coloring allows the kites to reflect the sun's brilliant hues quite effectively. Because dying agents are highly absorbent, even small quantities can color large surfaces with smooth, fresh-looking colors. These dyes are highly soluble, however, so care must be exercised. A recent development has been the production of colorants which are relatively stable when pressed with a hot iron after application.

Kite painting involves a variety of techniques, including traditional *hanga* woodblock printing, hand painting over block prints, or batik wax painting, which yields especially beautiful results on airborne kites. The wax-covered portions give off a resplendent glow.

Colorants closer at hand include poster paints, although these call for a light touch as they tend to blotch.

The transparency of vinyl has expanded the frontiers of kite decorating. Even the kite frame can be seen nestled in a blue sky. For three-dimensional kites in particular, vinyl enlarges the range of aesthetic effects far beyond the capacities of mere paper and cloth.

To color vinyl, use fast-drying felt-tipped pens or special vinyl paints and lacquer sprays, which produce especially nice reds and silvers. Spraying initially causes the vinyl to wrinkle, but this is only temporary. Pre-colored vinyl film is also effective.

## FRAMES AND GLUES

Bamboo, light and sturdy but highly flexible, is the traditional material used for Chinese and Japanese kite frames. In a later section we will learn how to build bamboo frames. For many kite enthusiasts, however, bamboo is simply not readily available, and in this case, cypress stripping is a perfectly adequate substitute.

Cypress stripping can be found in hobby shops or stores that carry materials for model plane and dollhouse construction. When choosing your cypress, select sturdy, straight, vertically grained pieces. Always examine them carefully to make sure they are strong.

Bond wood glue should be used for joining wood to paper. Vinyl glue should be used to attach vinyl sheeting to the frame. Note that if you use polyethylene instead of vinyl, it will not adhere to the glue, and must be taped instead.

## SKETCHING KITE PATTERNS

When designing any three-dimensional kite, whether based on square, circular, or triangular shapes, it is essential to think in terms of cubic figures. Sketch your ideas on paper as often as you like, always keeping in mind the fundamental principles of kite aerodynamics: lift, drag, and stability.

Once you've chosen a shape, it is time to draft the pattern. The most efficient use of materials will be achieved by adapting the size of your kite to the scale of the materials most readily available.

On the following pages are shown some ideas for kite designs, all building on the basic geometrical shapes of square, triangle, and circle, in increasingly intricate arrangements.

SKETCH PATTERNS FOR SQUARE, TRIANGULAR, AND CIRCULAR KITES

| | | |
|---|---|---|
| 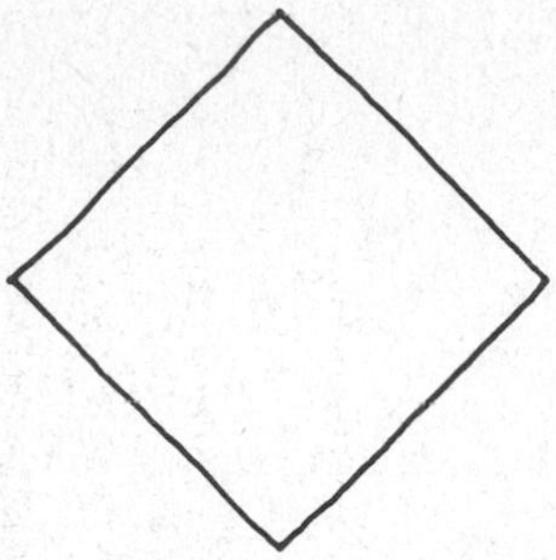 | 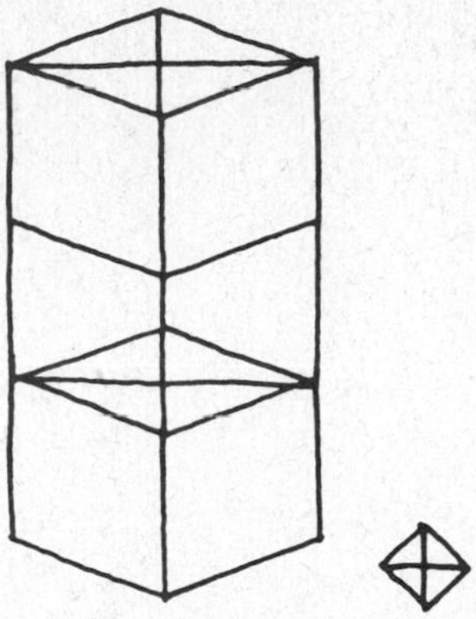 | 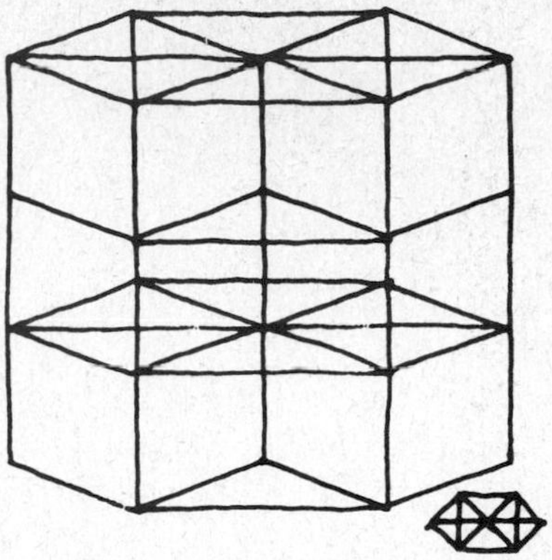 |
| square | ◇ · 2 | ◇ · 4 |
| 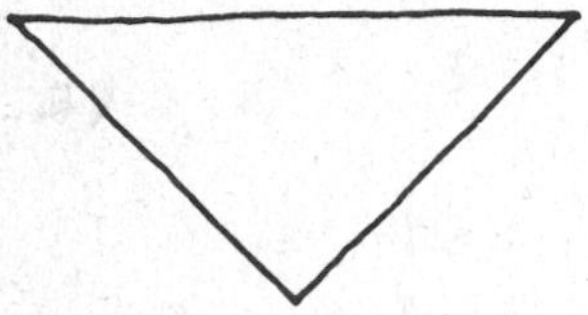 | 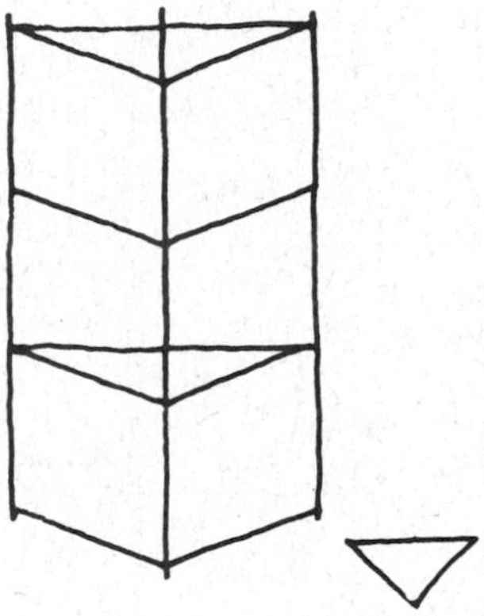 | 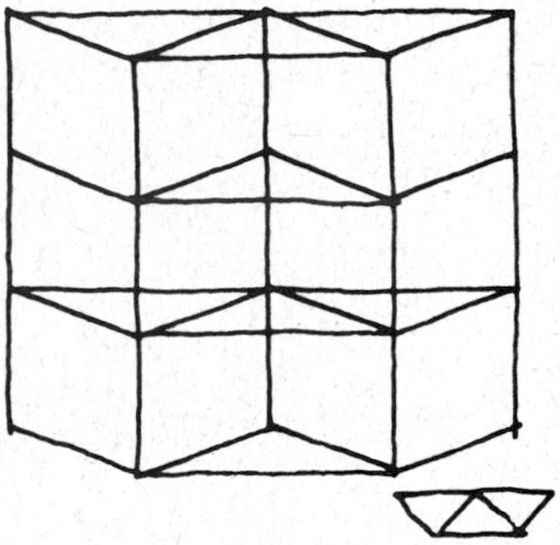 |
| triangle | ▽ · 2 | ▽ · 4 |
| 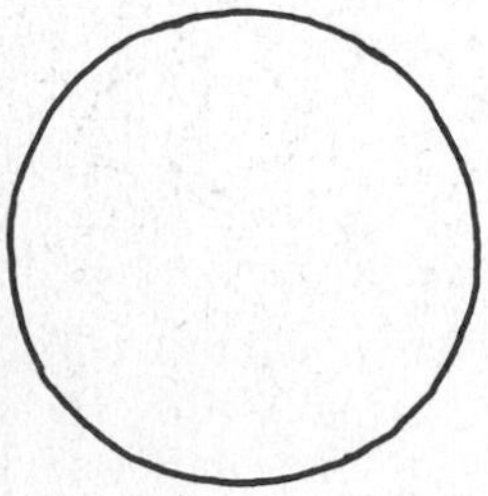 | 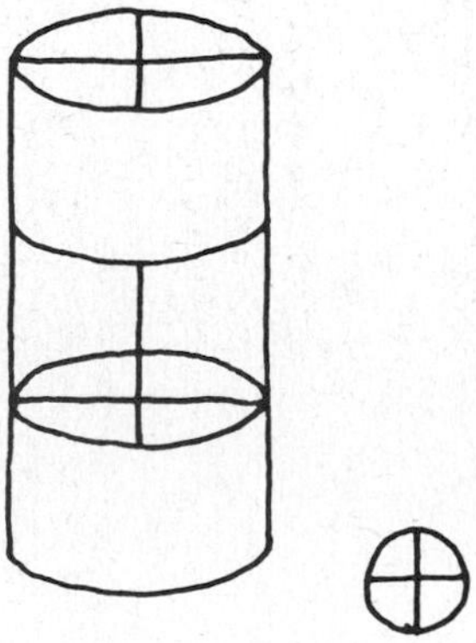 | 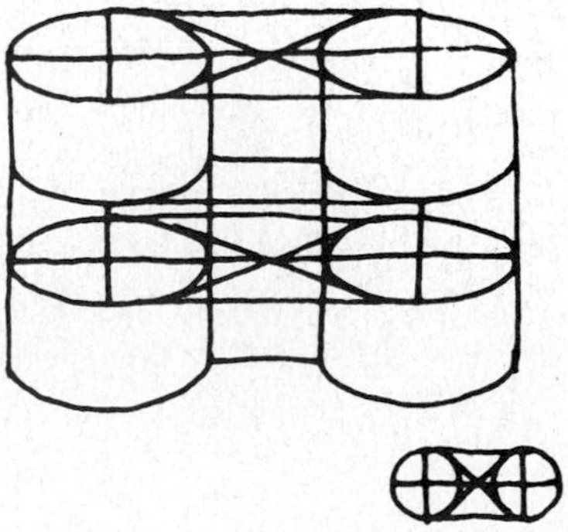 |
| circle | ○ · 2 | ○ · 4 |

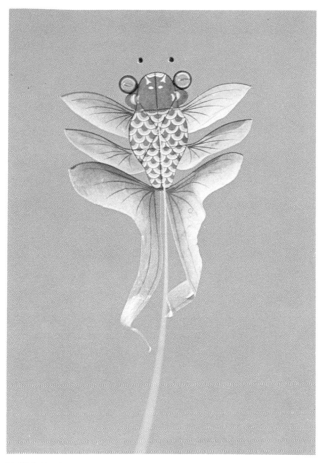

Goldfish kite from China. Chinese bamboo crafts-manship is highly refined, as the perfectly symmetrical yet infinitely intricate contours of this kite demonstrate. The secret of this amazing precision: a single piece of bamboo is fashioned into a pattern, then carefully split into two to produce a completely symmetrical frame. The structure is covered with soft paper to allow the fins to oscillate, conveying the impression of a fish swimming gracefully in the sky.

Puffer kite from the United States (see page 118 for diagram)

Trump kite. Two extra units are added on each side of the basic kite, for a total of eight panels each on the top and bottom, to produce this interesting variation.

Sting Ray kite from the United States. When sky-borne, the Sting Ray puts to fullest use the advantages of its plastic vinyl covering. The eyes, printed on adhesive seals, combine with its free design to give it a purposeful expression.

Jewel kite from Thailand. Circular kites are generally relatively unstable fliers, but this one maintains excellent equilibrium thanks to the liberation of its contours from the usual constraints imposed by the frame.

Jumbo kite from Hong Kong. Like the Puffer, this kite is inflated from a side of the tail wing. Transparent vinyl is spread over the space extending from the wings to the body to provide added lift.

Space-Bird from the United States. This light-cloth three-dimensional bird kite can be conveniently folded up and carried off by removing a single horizontal spar; its wing spread is 160cm.

Indonesian kite. Like the Thai cobra and peacock kites, this also incorporates a tail in its overall design, and displays the brilliant colors of its homeland.

Centipede kite from China (see pages 121, 122 for diagram)

Cobra kite from Thailand (see page 123 for diagram)

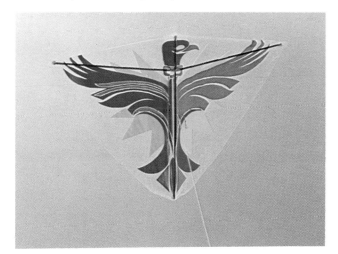

Bird kite from France. Bird-spaced kites are to be found in all countries, yet there is something distinctively French about this brilliantly colored species, which suggests a coat of arms that has taken to the air.

Flower basket from China. The lilies and tulips sticking out of this overladen flower basket in the sky make this elaborate creation appear a bit off-balance.

Tiger kite: a creative variation of the basic box kite (see page 108 for diagram)

Cubic kite (see page 104 for diagram)

Space medusa (see page 112 for diagram)

Mach 9 kite (see page 110 for diagram)

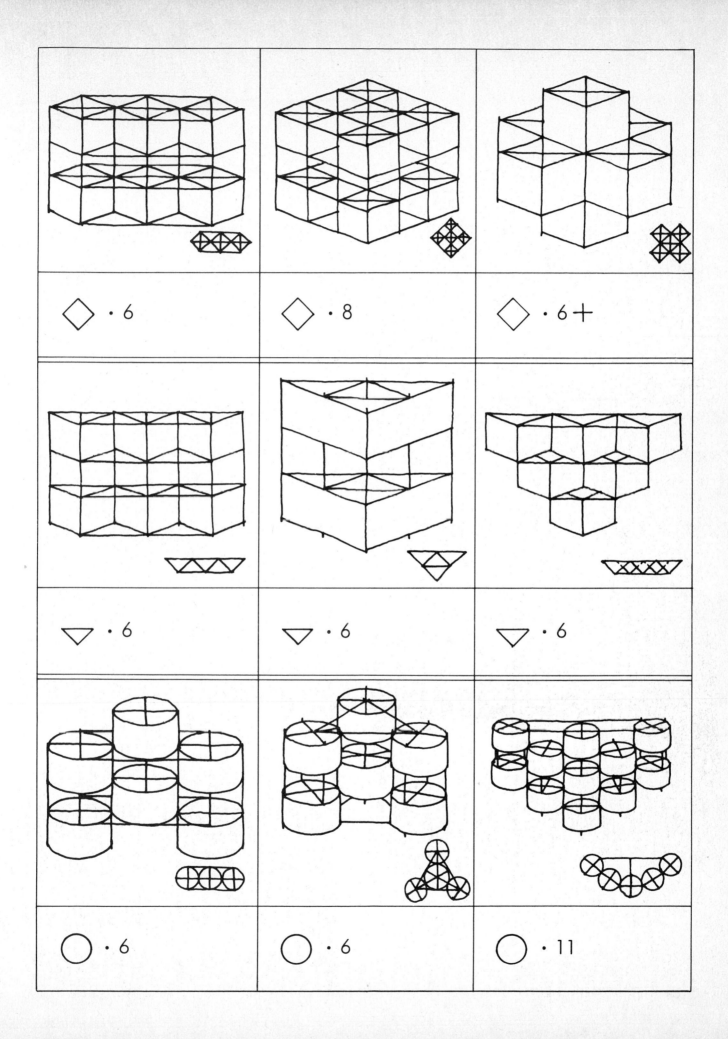

◇ · 6

◇ · 8

◇ · 6+

▽ · 6

▽ · 6

▽ · 6

○ · 6

○ · 6

○ · 11

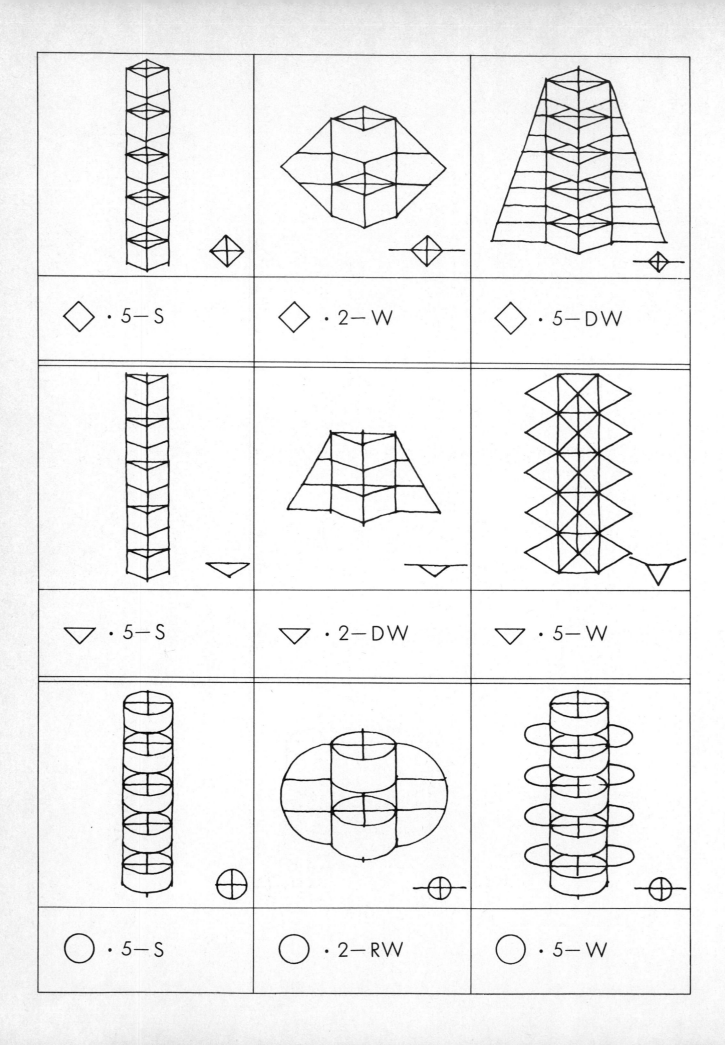

◇ · 5—S          ◇ · 2—W          ◇ · 5—DW

▽ · 5—S          ▽ · 2—DW          ▽ · 5—W

◯ · 5—S          ◯ · 2—RW          ◯ · 5—W

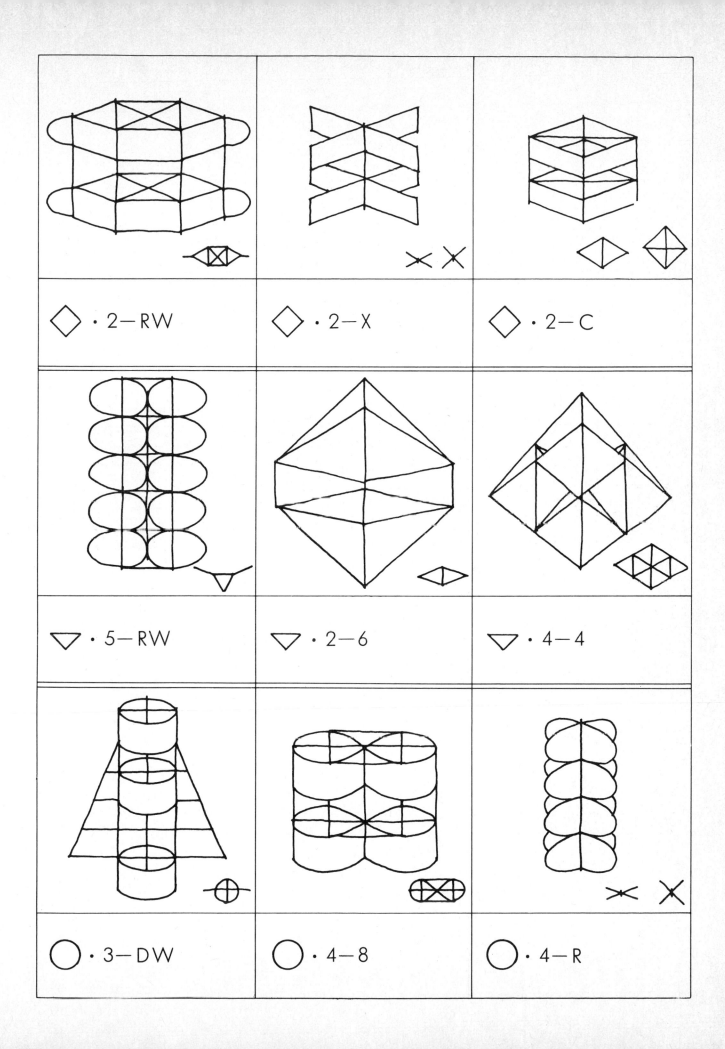

◇ · 2—RW   ◇ · 2—X   ◇ · 2—C

▽ · 5—RW   ▽ · 2—6   ▽ · 4—4

◯ · 3—DW   ◯ · 4—8   ◯ · 4—R

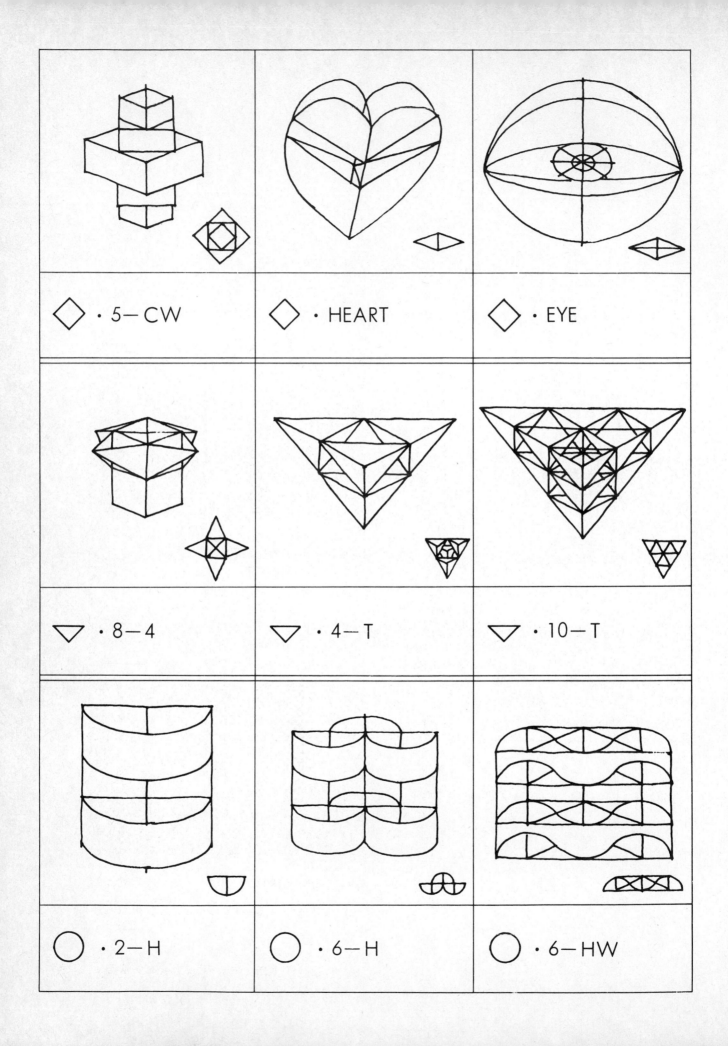

◇ · 5—CW          ◇ · HEART          ◇ · EYE

▽ · 8—4          ▽ · 4—T          ▽ · 10—T

◯ · 2—H          ◯ · 6—H          ◯ · 6—HW

# The Basic Box Kite

The construction of the basic three-dimensional box kite provides us with a model for triangular, cylindrical, and other shaped kites of our own inspiration. Collapsible and portable, it weighs 160g, including the frame, vinyl, paper, and string. I used the full lengths of 90cm cypress strips for the vertical spines, and half-lengths (45cm) for the crosspieces. My vinyl sheeting was 30cm wide, so I set my wing span at 28cm, allowing a 1cm margin for glue at each end. For this and the other kites diagrammed, I have indicated the wing spread, wing load, and weight, so you can select the proper kite line and flying conditions. For calculations of this information, see the Appendix.

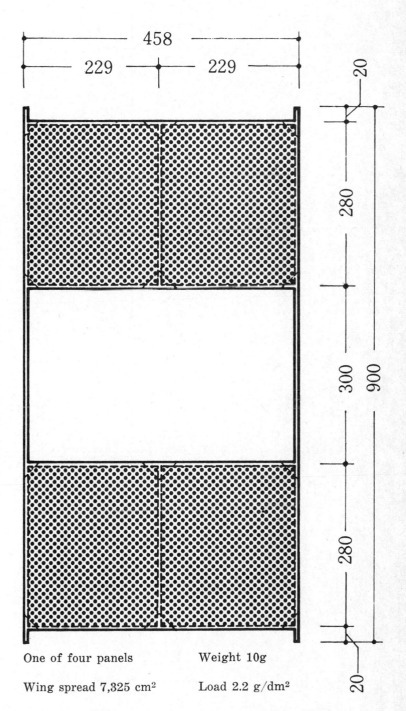

One of four panels          Weight 10g

Wing spread 7,325 cm²       Load 2.2 g/dm²

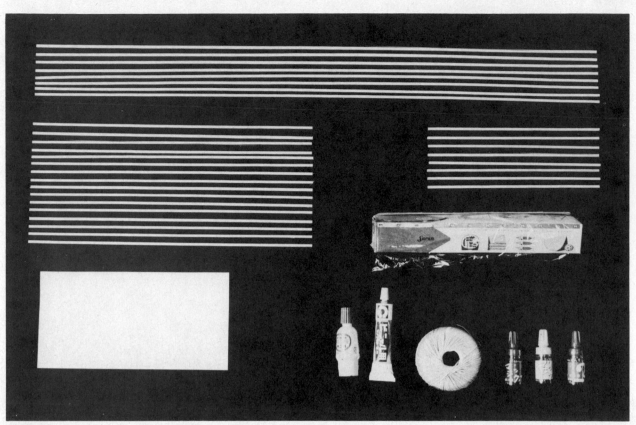

Materials for the basic box kite

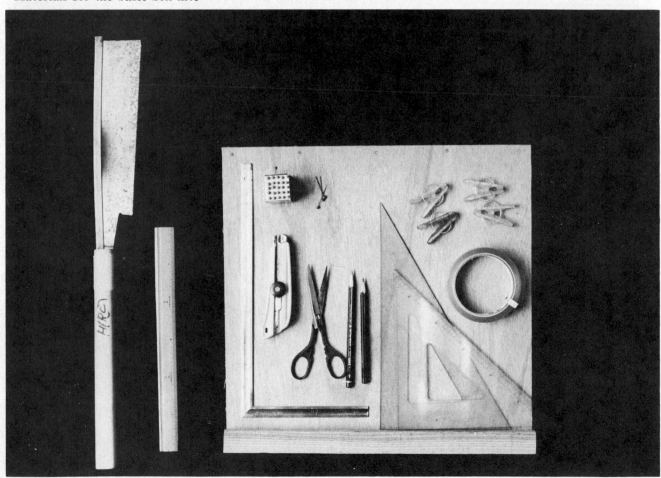

Tools for the basic box kite

## MATERIALS

| | |
|---|---|
| 8 cypress strips | 4mm × 4mm × 900mm |
| 16 cypress strips | 4mm × 4mm × 450mm |
| 8 cypress strips | 4mm × 4mm × 272mm |
| | or ⅛-inch white-wood dowels |
| Kent paper | 12cm × 36cm |

Vinyl (0.01 thickness) or polyethylene film (0.03)

Bond glue for use with wood

Vinyl glue or double-faced adhesive tape

Large vinyl sheet to cover working board

Felt-tipped coloring pens

No. 10 kite string (4m) (for bridle)

No. 20 count 5 string (for flying line)

You may also want to use a slender, nonelastic string to lash together the panel assembly and to make cross strings, which will reinforce it.

## TOOLS

Thin, small-toothed wood saw, ruler, carpenter's T-square, cutting knife, scissors, pencils, triangles, push pins, clothespins, cellophane tape, and a working board. The working board may be made from a veneer board about 45cm on each side. Nail a 3cm-wide strip of wood on both sides (above and below) of one edge of the board. The lower projection will allow you to fix the board more firmly against a desk or table edge, while the upper one will be convenient for sawing and arranging materials.

## CONSTRUCTION

1. Line the strips up on the working board, and use the T-square to mark the cutting positions.

2. Hold the strips firmly together with one hand to prevent sliding, and saw gently but smoothly. With the proper blade, you should be able to cut them all at once. If no saw is available, cut the strips individually with the cutting knife, turning them as you cut.

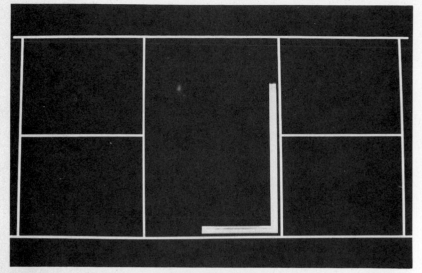

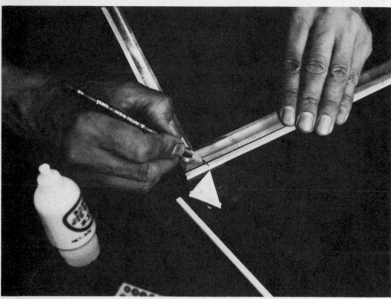

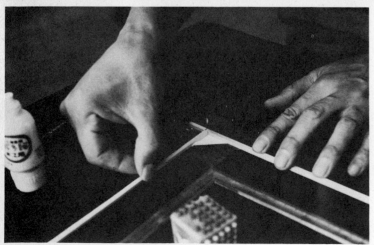

3. Spread out your materials on a level surface and assemble the strips to approximate each panel of the kite.

4. Measure, outline with a pencil and ruler, and cut the paper into ninety-six right triangles with 3cm sides. These will be used as reinforcements to insure that the frame angles are true. Keep them ready. At the same time, cut out and set aside forty-eight 5cm × 5cm squares of vinyl.

5. Mark off 2cm at each panel corner.

6. Use bond glue to attach the Kent paper reinforcements to the corners of the lower panels. Be sure to place the previously pre-

pared vinyl squares between the triangles and the working board to prevent them from sticking together. Vinyl is suitable for this purpose because ordinary glue will not adhere to it.

7. Apply bond wood glue to the tips of the cypress sticks to be joined.

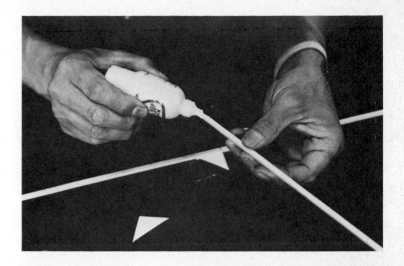

8. Next apply glue to the triangular reinforcements and paste them to the corners of the upper frame section, taking care that they do not slide.

9. Fix the glued triangles to the frame with push pins so that they will not move; let dry for 20–30 minutes.

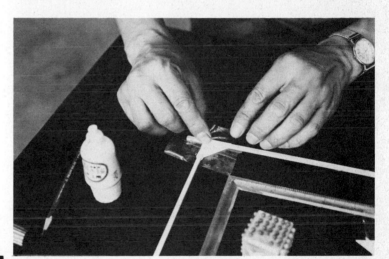

10. Follow the same procedure for each corner until you have assembled the four panels. Be sure that your corners form true right angles.

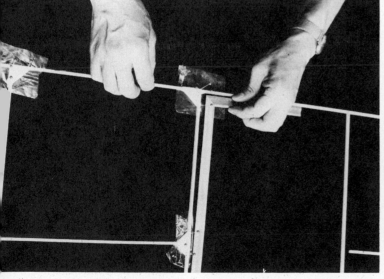

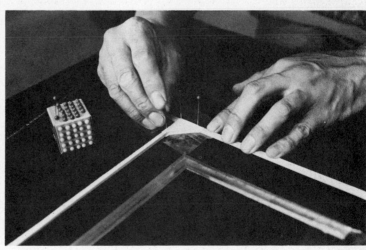

11. After the glue has dried, remove the pins; your panel frames are now ready for covering.

12. Spread out the vinyl sheeting, and ready it for pasting to the frame.

13. Apply vinyl glue to the frame. (If using polyethylene film, you will need double-faced adhesive tape.)

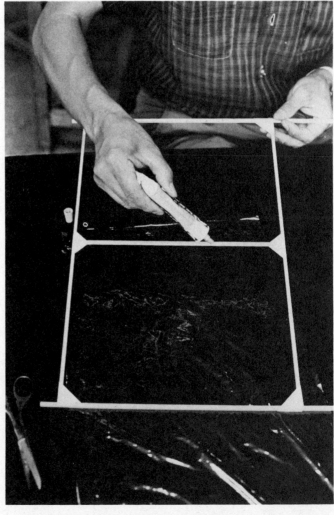

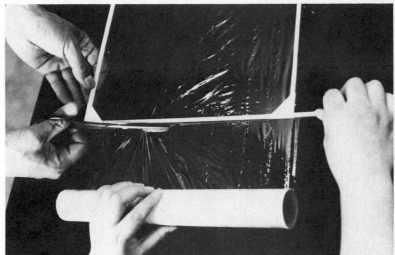

14. Glue the vinyl to the frame.

15. Cut the vinyl sheet from its roll, leaving a 1cm margin at the end.

16. Now apply vinyl glue to the remaining edge.

17. Attach the vinyl to this edge, wrapping the extra margin around it.

18. Color the completed panel. Try to make a design that will be visible from a distance, so you can recognize it in flight. Use whatever aids you like (ruler, triangle, compass, etc.) for the design. It is sometimes helpful to do a rough, full-size sketch on another piece of paper beforehand.

19. Apply your color as carefully and smoothly as possible.

20. Now assemble the frame, making sure that the edges to which the vinyl has been attached face out.

21. Use rubber bands or string to temporarily hold the four corners together while you tie the corner strips in place with thin kite string.

22. After tying one corner, extend the string (without cutting it) diagonally across the box cell and tie the opposite end. Make sure that the kite is square as you tie the corners together.

23. Attach cross strings (eight in all) above and below each panel. This will strengthen the kite's overall structure.

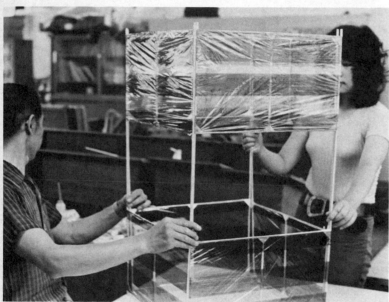

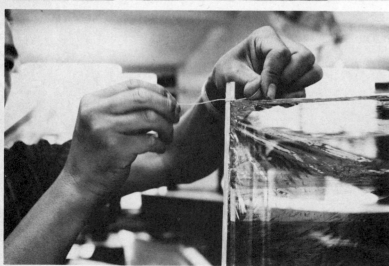

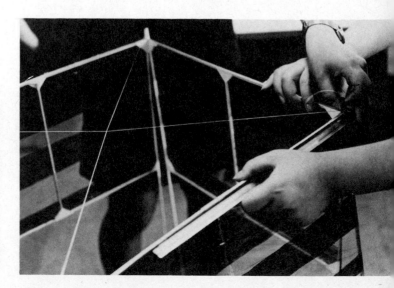

Examine the completed kite to see that it is straight and balanced. You may, if you like, adjust the lengths of the cross strings to obtain a rhombic shape. This will increase the kite's wing span, and make it easier to fly in a light breeze. For strong winds, you may want to construct a three-panel triangular kite. This produces the opposite effect of the diamond shape, reducing wing spread and allowing the triangular box form to withstand rather strong winds without cross-string support.

## BRIDLING

This box kite has a drag of about 1kg in a strong wind, for which No. 20 count 5 string should be adequate. An even thinner, lighter string would have less slack and permit the kite to fly farther and higher. The bridle for this kite should consist of two 2m lengths of No. 10 kite string, with one leg tied to the kite top and the other attached about two thirds of the way down. Use a vertical knot to secure the bridle to the kite.

The bridling point should be located at a point about one sixth of the way down from the kite top. Connect the two ends using a simple knot, and make a loop for attaching the flying line. The kite will fly differently depending on where the bridle center is set relative to the kite's vertical axis. In a strong enough breeze, a single line attached directly to the kite top is adequate.

## LAUNCHING AND FLYING

After you've tied the flying line to the bridle loop, it is time to make a test flight. Hold the flying line at about eye-level, and position yourself relative to the wind. As you begin to let out enough line, there is always the danger of the kite's crashing to the ground; but if your kite is structurally balanced and free of distortions, it should prove a stable flier.

Have a friend walk the kite as far downwind as the lay of the land permits and hold the kite ready for launching. The launcher should take care not to reverse the kite top and bottom, and make sure that there is no danger of the bridle getting tangled with the kite. When a sufficient gust of wind arises, have the launcher let go of the kite as you take in as much line as possible. If wind conditions are adequate, the kite should rise steadily.

Once the kite is up in the air and maintaining its equilibrium, let out some more line. This will cause the kite to sink, as pulling on the line again will cause the kite to rise. Alternate this reeling in and letting out of the line until the kite has found a windstream able to sustain it at a proper flying altitude. You will know it has found its orbit when feeding out string no longer causes it to descend.

There are times when running with a kite might seem to be called for, but as a general rule (giant kites are a special case) kites such as the one we have constructed demand the kind of attention that makes running with one's eyes directed skyward hazardous rather than helpful.

Kiting is a sport that can be enjoyed at any time of year as long as there is a decent wind blowing. Take your kite and fly it at the seashore or in the mountains. It is all right to fly it in nearby vacant lots or open spaces, but do not go kiting on roads or in places where there are buildings, tall trees, telephone or electric wires, etc. If your kite or line gets entangled in high wires, do not try to yank it free; cut the line off at your end. In general, try to avoid such situations by thinking like an airplane pilot, taking careful note of the wind direction, the topography, and prevailing conditions in the surrounding area.

If you feel the wind change and sense danger while flying your kite, wait for the wind to calm down before reeling in your line. Do not remain in one spot as you reel in; this may cause your line to tangle. Instead, move slowly as you pull, dispersing the reeled-in line on the ground as you walk. Be sure to handle your kite carefully once it has been safely retrieved. Repair even the slightest damage in anticipation of your next flight.

A *dojingoshi* kite caught in the branches of a Zelkova tree

# Making a Gunya-gunya Kite

*Gunya-gunya* (literally, "flabby" or "limp") kites, also known as poster or flexible kites, fly splendidly without tails at wind speeds of 3–15m. While their construction is simple (two strips of cypress and a handy polyethylene bag) it does require a certain amount of precision.

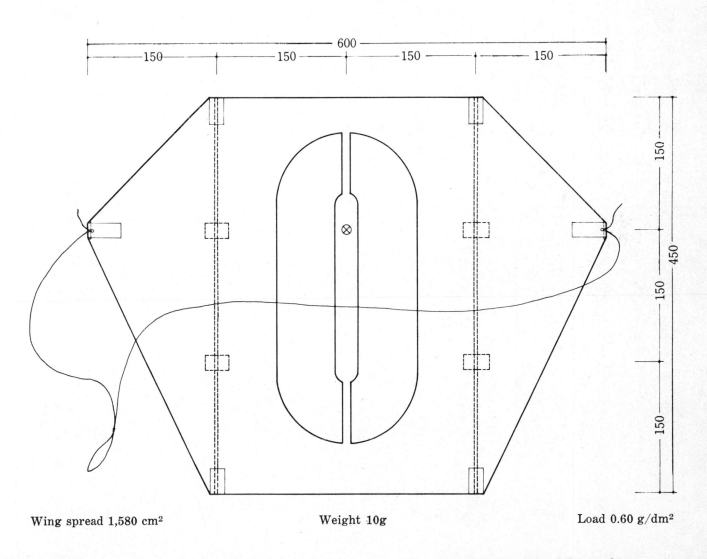

Wing spread 1,580 cm²        Weight 10g        Load 0.60 g/dm²

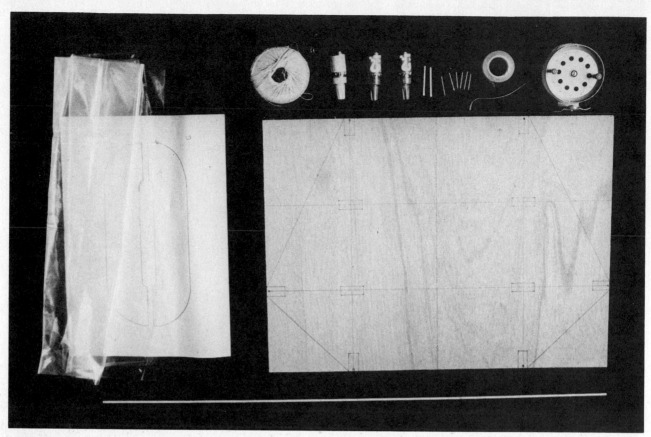

Materials for the *gunya-gunya* kite

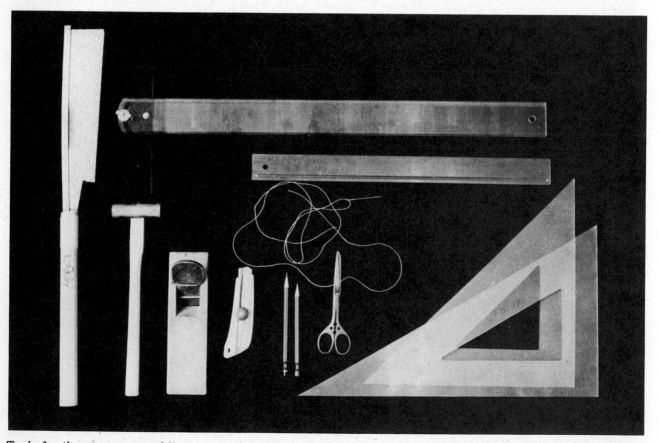

Tools for the *gunya-gunya* kite

## MATERIALS

1 polyethylene bag (0.03) with interior dimensions of at least 600mm × 450mm

1 cypress strip    4mm × 4mm × 900mm or 1 ⅛-inch white-wood dowel

Vinyl tape or Texcel tape    about 600mm

1 toothpick or matchstick

Hemp line (for bridle)    about 1.5m

No. 20 count 3 flax sewing thread or No. 40 count lace thread (for flying line)

Felt-tipped coloring pens

Thick pattern paper or plywood

6 nails

Sketching paper

Reel (a fishing reel is fine)

## TOOLS

Knife, sewing needle, scissors, small plane (optional), small-toothed saw, hammer, ruler, workboard.

## CONSTRUCTION

1. Draw an accurate full-scale outline on thick pattern paper or plywood.

2. Cut off the four corners with the saw.

3. Spread the polyethylene bag under the pattern board, and hammer nails through the board and bag in the six places indicated (top, bottom, and sides) to prevent the bag from sliding. Be sure there is a workboard underneath to avoid damage to furniture. The nail holes made at this time will serve as guide marks during the assembly stage.

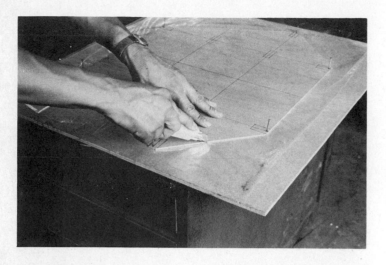

4. Following the pattern, cut the polyethylene bag.

5. Carefully remove the corners, making sure that the material has been completely cut through.

6. It is possible to cut as many as forty sheets at the same time. Such multiple cutting is easier, however, if you use polyethylene bags larger than the pattern board.

7. Cut two strips of cypress 450mm long by carefully sawing the 900mm strip in half. Mark each piece in thirds (150mm).

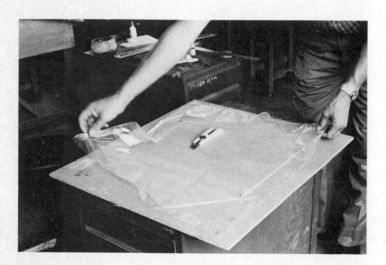

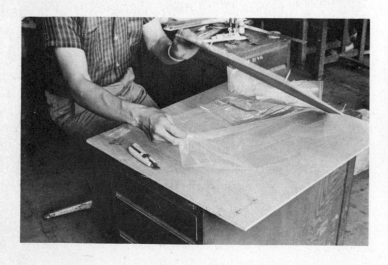

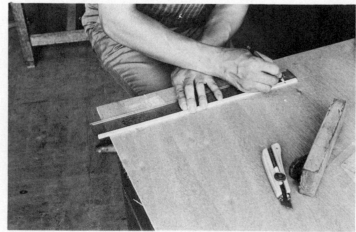

8. Holding the two strips together and parallel, shave them so that they taper down toward the tip. You may use a small plane to shave them down.

9. Repeat the procedure for the opposite ends.

10. Prepare ten 60mm strips of vinyl tape.

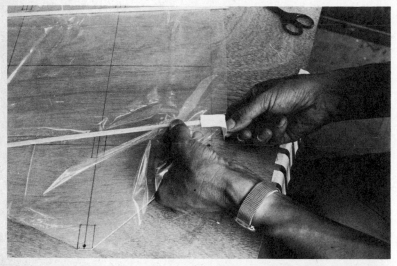

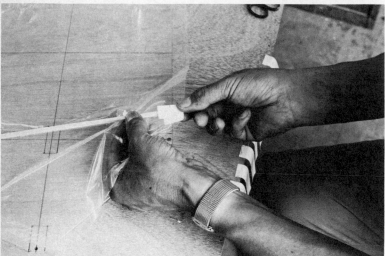

11. Lay the wood strips vertically from the top to the bottom of the polyethylene covering, making sure that they lie over the nail hole guide marks. Fold the 60mm strips of tape over the ends of the strips to hold them in place. (If you leave the polyethylene over the pattern, you will be able to use the marks on the pattern as guides while you work.)

12. Press down firmly on the tape.

13. Place vinyl tape over the wood strips at the vertical third-way point markings. As you work, be sure to smooth out the polyethylene so that there are no wrinkles when the frame is attached to the bag.

14. Continue to attach the vinyl strips in the eight places indicated on the pattern, taking care not to push the wood out of place.

15. Cut the matchstick (or toothpick) into two pieces, each as long as the width of the tape.

16. Lay one of the match lengths across the middle of a piece of vinyl tape.

17. Fold the tape over the polyethylene sheet at its right-hand side angle so that the enclosed matchstick is at the outer edge. Repeat the same procedure for the left-hand side.

18. Thread the sewing needle with the bridle line, and push it firmly through the tape and the enclosed matchstick. Then, using the other end of the same thread, repeat the procedure on the other side of the polyethylene sheet. The bridle length (1.5m) is two and a half times the kite width.

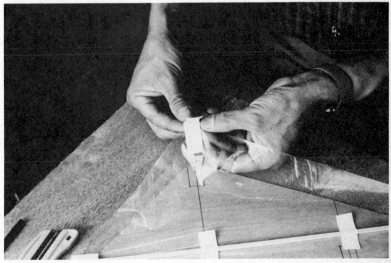

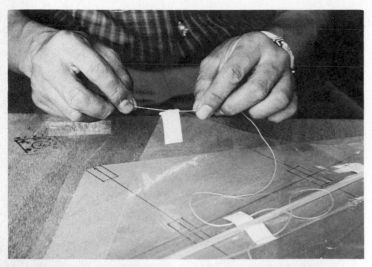

19. Leave an extra 40mm or so, and tie the line securely. This will prevent loosening and facilitate adjustment and regulation of the kite's flying position later on.

20. To set the bridle, fold the kite in half, with the two wood strips carefully placed on top of each other. Now fold the bridle into two equal lengths. The side with the frame will be your kite's backside.

21. Using a simple knot at the halfway point in the bridle, make a loop for the flying line to go through.

22. Prepare your design on the sketching paper and place it under the polyethylene. Now color your kite with the felt-tipped pens. Try to keep your design more than 50mm from the vertical supports, as these sections tend to be hidden from sight during flight. You should aim for a design that will be visible from at least 100m.

23. Now attach the flying line securely and make your test flight.

24. A fishing reel is ideal for handling large amounts of line.

25. If you wish, you can check the flying line's breaking strength (the number of grams of tensile strength it will support) with a spring balance.

The proper bridle leg length is crucial. It is sometimes possible to restore perfect alignment to a kite that has tipped over merely by adding a hitch to the bridle knot on the inclined side.

Once you have verified the kite's stability, you are ready to fly. Do not hesitate to give

your kite a substantial amount of line. With 1,000m, it should vanish in the clouds, giving the impression of a line hanging by itself from the sky.

It is also fun to form a kite train by using a thicker line and attaching several other *gunya-gunya* kites at 100m intervals. Launch each additional kite separately on about 10m of flying line before attaching it to the main line. A kite train guarantees maximum height and distance without inducing sag, but only if your line is strong enough to sustain the pull of the lengthening train. *Gunya-gunya* kite trains also lend themselves well to "sky writing." Paint one letter on each kite and spell a word—L-O-V-E, R-A-I-N-B-O-W, S-K-Y. Take care not to fly kite trains too high as there is a real danger of collision with airplanes.

## THE PROPER PROPORTIONS

The *gunya-gunya* kite has a basic vertical-horizontal ratio of 3:4. Both larger and smaller kites, which fly equally well, may be constructed on the basis of this model. The diagrams on the facing page illustrate other possible proportions. Kites 1, 2, and 3 suggest variations which can be achieved by increasing the vertical component relative to the horizontal but keeping the tie point set at one third of the total height. All three are stable fliers. Kite 4 shows how even bigger kites can be produced by increasing the number of center surface units and the number of bridles used.

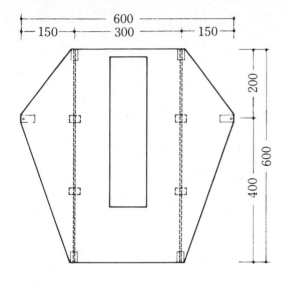

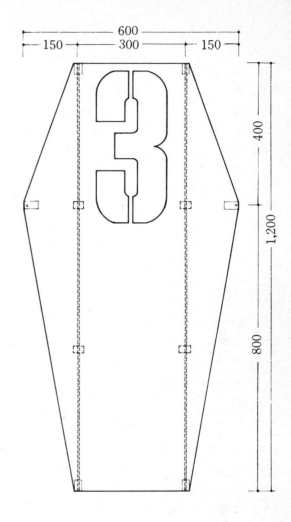

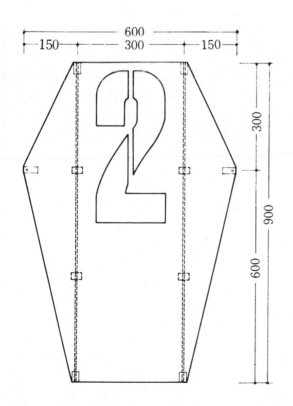

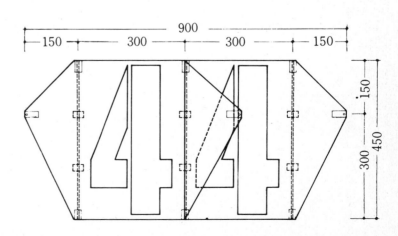

# Building a Bamboo Frame

One of the primary reasons the kite developed as it did in China and Japan was the availability of bamboo, a light but sturdy and highly flexible material that proved ideal for kite frame construction. While it is not so readily available in the United States as in Japan, persistent kite-fanciers can usually secure a small supply with which to construct their own bamboo frames (see Appendix for some suggested sources). The advantages as well as the beauty of a genuine bamboo frame make the extra effort rewarding.

There are many varieties of bamboo, but the strongest and most suitable is long-jointed bamboo with low and relatively far apart nodes.

Bamboo stems should ideally be cut between November, around the time of the first frost, and January. Bamboo cut at other times of the year may be infested with insects.

There are also regional variations. Bamboo from warm southern Kyushu is especially high in quality. The particular variety used for the Nagasaki *hata* from that region is grown in Yamaga (Kumamoto Prefecture) and considered to be among the best in the world. In Japan's cold northeast, high-quality cypress is used in preference to bamboo.

## CONSTRUCTION

Few would challenge the superiority of bamboo for kite frame construction, but its handling does demand a certain degree of competence. To do your kite justice, therefore, you will probably want to work under the direction of someone experienced in cutting bamboo.

1. Cut the bamboo to measure with a bamboo saw, distinguishing (for future reference) the top (branches) from the bottom (roots).

2. Using a bamboo cutting knife, split the stalk in half, beginning at the top and working all the way down to the bottom. Set the bottom end on a thick tree stump or block to avoid damaging the bamboo extremities or your cutting knife.

3. Now repeat the process with each of the two halves, cutting straight down the middle. Continue cutting each new length in half.

4. When you have eight pieces, remove the nodes.

5. Now comes the hard stripping. In order to split the stalk into sixteen and then thirty-two strips, hold each length firmly between your left thumb and index finger; with your right hand, wedge the knife into the edge of the bamboo and push down all the way to the other end.

6. Be sure to keep a tight grip on the bamboo, as this will ensure that the knife is sandwiched by the bamboo. Likewise, always stop cutting at a safe distance from your left hand. Jackknives and kitchen knives are dangerous and best avoided.

7. If you find you are cutting unevenly, raise or lower your cutting blade a bit, simultaneously adjusting your finger or thumb pressure.

8. The same procedure applies when slicing the outer rim. This is a very delicate operation, and it is not advised for beginners.

Snow falling on freshly cut long-jointed bamboo, bundled and ready to transport for use

The width and thickness desired will depend on the size and structure of the kite you are going to construct. For a kite to be covered by a single sheet of *nishinouchi* paper, a thickness of about 1.5mm will do, although the strips for the center spine and the top spars to which cross strings will be attached should be a shade thicker. For a kite with a covering of three sheets of *nishinouchi* paper, use 2mm-thick stripping. A kite with only a few spars and spines is best made with strips of 3–6mm thickness. Depending on the use to which the kite is to be put, the bamboo strips may require additional shaping and trimming.

A rectangular kite about 2m square will require 2cm-wide strips of bamboo, peeled down to a thickness of about 3mm. The larger the kite, the thicker its "skeleton" should be. A giant kite of about 4–5m on a side will use a whole round bamboo shaft for its major frame components. The fact that the shaft interior is hollow helps to reduce the weight of giant kites and allows the excellence of the bamboo to be used to full advantage.

# Sky Climbers and Hummers

Once a kite has gained its maximum altitude and is flying smoothly, its line may appear as an arc suspended in the sky, or rather like a circus tightrope beckoning us to climb it to the heavens. Various kite attachments can allow us to experience, albeit vicariously, the feeling of actual ascension up that line. Generally referred to as sky climbers, they may include a variety of forms and devices, such as pinwheels, vents, parachutes, or monstrous butterflies with flapping wings, known as winged missiles in their native Okinawa. In addition, you can attach noisemakers called *unari*, or hummers. In their wails, cries, buzzes, etc., one can hear the voice of the enslaved wind, harnessed as a source of power for the airborne kite. Let us examine some of these intriguing devices to see how we can further enhance our enjoyment of kites.

## SKY SPINNERS

A simple climber can be made by cutting a piece of Kent paper into a geometric shape and then cutting and folding it along the lines indicated in the photograph. Insert a straw through the center hole, and make a thin slit from the hole to the outer edge. Pass the flying line through the slit; then tape it closed again. The climber should spin its way up the line.

The spinning climber on the left in the photograph is made of two crisscrossed bamboo slats with a straw attached to their point of intersection, and with slightly cupped discs of Kent paper glued to the slat ends. This may be sent up the line in the same manner as the others. Larger kites may feature an umbrella climber. Once the open umbrella catches the wind, it swiftly whirls up the line. When it hits the kite bridle, it closes and shimmies back down. Other devices include cones or bags that burst open and release a shower of confetti, and parachutes that open and fall when they strike the bridle base. Use your ingenuity and develop other types of climbers.

## BUTTERFLY CLIMBERS

In Okinawa, large kites sometimes have big butterfly climbers made of bamboo. These open and close their wings as they slide up and down the flying line. When the forward spring mechanism hits the bridle knot, the bamboo bow in front is released, causing the string attached to it to slacken, the butterfly's wings to fold, and the entire mechanism to slide down the line. A sure people-pleaser, this particular yellow butterfly is the creation of Seiichi Nigaki of Naha, Okinawa.

## MATERIALS
1 strip long-jointed bamboo    270mm × 12mm
2 strips small bamboo    700mm × 2mm
*Washi* paper (4–5g)
Hemp line
Colored poster bond paper
Wire
Glue

An assortment of sky climbers and spinners you can easily build

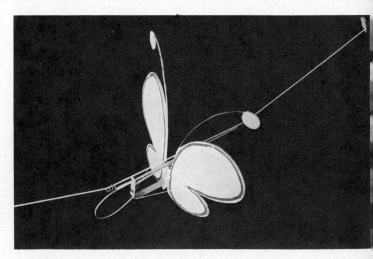

Butterfly rocket, a decorative sky climber

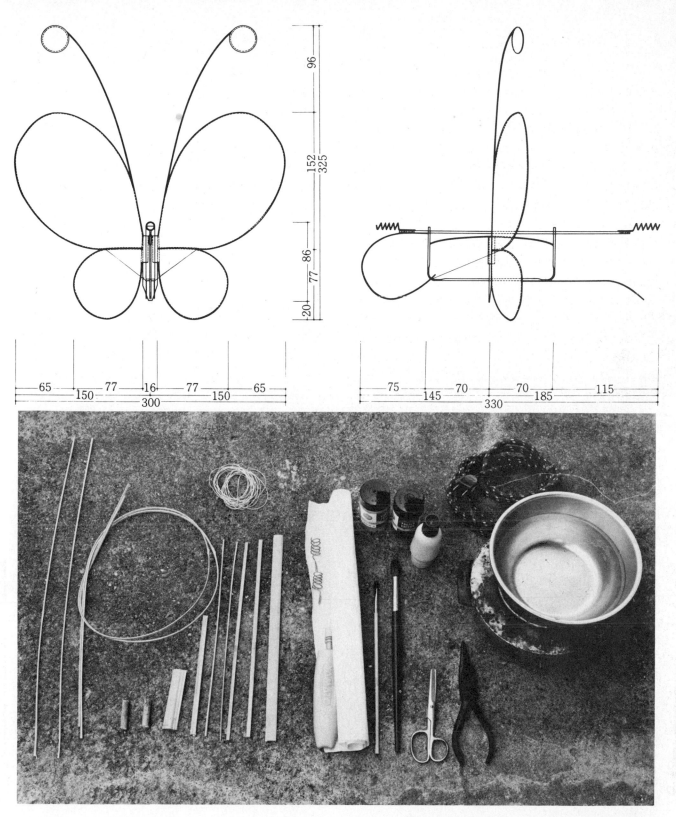

Materials and tools for the butterfly rocket

## TOOLS

Knife or saw (to cut bamboo), scissors, ruler, pencil, plane, two kitchen pots, awl, jeweler's or other fine-toothed saw.

## CONSTRUCTION

1. Cut off a 270mm × 12mm strip of bamboo.

2. Split it into 2mm-thick strips.

3. Mark off the sections that are to be bent, 65mm from each end of the 270mm strip.

4. Shave or plane these sections down.

5. Place the strips in a pot of boiling water and bend at right angles at the points indicated. You will have to compensate for the bamboo's tendency to reassert its natural structure by bending it slightly beyond 90°.

6. Place the bent portions in cold water and let harden.

7. Use an awl to bore holes through the ends of the bent sections for the central shaft to pass through.

8. Make the wings by bending and tying 700mm × 2mm bamboo strips into arcs as shown in the photo. Glue them to cylindrical sections of the small bamboo, which will serve as the hinges. Also apply glue to the wing junction to keep the string from coming loose.

9. Bore a hole in the central section; this will contain the hinge fittings.

10. Enlarge the opening with a jeweler's saw. The central section is now ready for assembly.

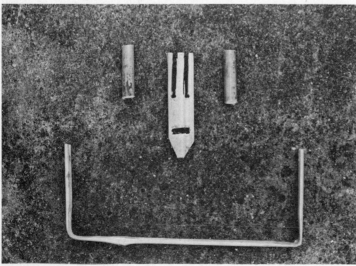

11. Coil the wire into springs, folding back the ends which are to be attached to the central shaft.

12. Make holes in the main body section to allow the taut inside string to be released as the bamboo bow (lower left of photo 14) is sprung when it bangs into the bridle knot.

13. Attach and color the *nishinouchi* paper. When placing the butterfly on the flying line, make sure that the line also passes through the spring coils. If desired, attach a confetti-throwing device to the elastic bamboo bow and set it to release a confetti shower when the wings fold.

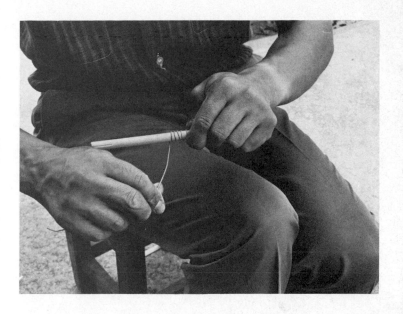

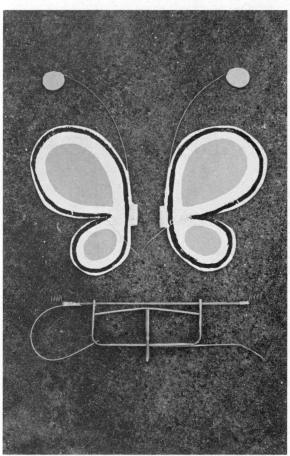

# HUMMERS

Hummers are the voice of the wind. The use of hummers dates back to fairly ancient times, a fact attested to by one Chinese term meaning kite, *fon tien*, or wind harp. There is no doubt that the people who first conceived the fine idea of attaching noisemakers to kites to enhance that illusion did so with full awareness of the kite's special, intimate relationship to the wind.

Hummers are generally bows of string or thin bamboo attached to the top of the kite like a set of antlers. The big hummer in the photograph below is made of a piece of bamboo 73cm long, 8mm wide, and 5mm thick. The ends are tapered to 3mm, and the outer edge of the strip is turned inward. The string is made of 5mm-wide thinly stripped rattan shaved down to a thickness of about 0.3mm (slightly thicker than a postcard). The ends are fitted with 2cm-long segments of thin 8mm-diameter bamboo to which the rattan bow-string is fastened.

You may vary the sound your hummer produces by attaching a 3–6cm-wide strip of thin *washi* or wax paper around the hummer string and cutting slits in the paper at 2–3cm intervals.

Rattan can break easily when dry, so take care to moisten it before mounting. In spite of this hummer's fairly solid construction, it is advisable to reinforce the structure with string to prevent it from falling apart. In addition to rattan, hummer strings may be made of flat, finely stripped whalebone, flat elastic cord or tape, or colored vinyl wrapping tape.

This type of large hummer is attached to kites measuring 46cm × 80cm, the size of a rectangular kite covered with two and a half sheets of *nishinouchi* paper. The hummer is fastened to the rectangular kite's top corner protrusions with thick rubber bands. To keep the bow from wobbling, tie its center to the middle of the second vertical spine. The size of the hummer should be in proportion to the size of the kite.

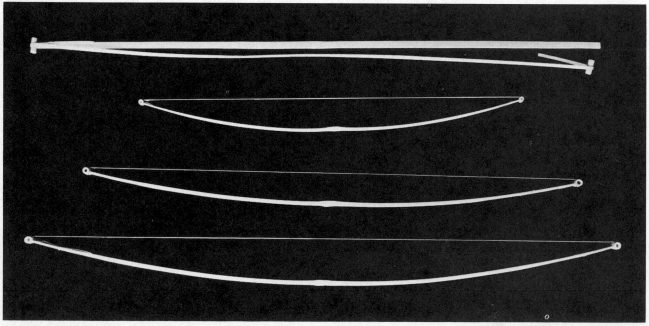

Hummers, voices of the wind

# 4
# Creative Kites: Sculpting the Sky

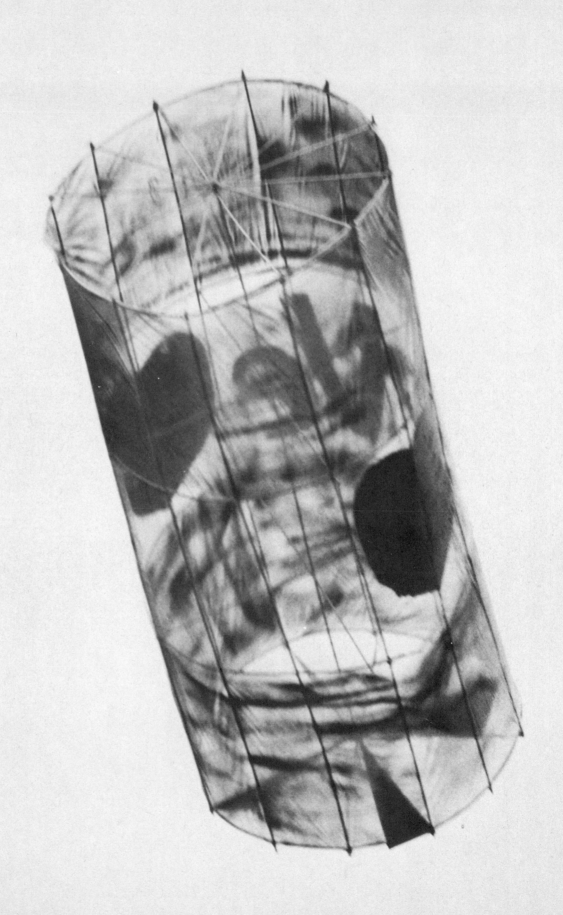

Man first attempted to reach the heavens by imitating birds in flight, an approach which, at that stage of human development, was unreliable at best. It was only later, after analyzing flight into its various components of lift, drag, and propulsion and then integrating them into a workable theory, that he finally achieved success. One would be safe in saying that, on the whole, the same principles that led to the invention of the airplane apply to three-dimensional kites. And yet, these toy-like creations would seem to derive their special meaning not only from their ability to fly but from the relentless pursuit of new

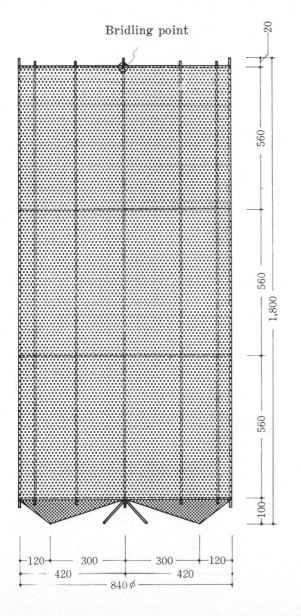

Bridling point

imaginative design they inspire. Just as the airplane advances through history in its unceasing quest for functionality, so does the three-dimensional kite advance toward as yet uncharted areas of structural design and creativity.

Some of this progress is illustrated by the models of creative box and flat kites presented on the following pages.

## DRUMCAN KITE

Thanks to the four-spoked pinwheel mechanism at the bottom of the large cylinder, this kite revolves like a merry-go-round as it climbs. The bridling point is centered in the circular

Wing spread 28,224 cm²

Weight 650g

Load 2.30 g/dm²

top, and the device is equipped with sturdy fishing-type anti-twist metal fittings to prevent the flying line from becoming entangled. The drumcan will spin spectacularly right above your head, provided the wind is strong enough.

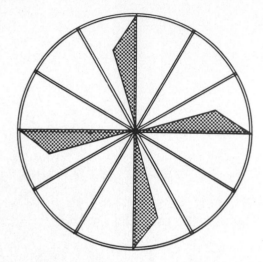

The symbol ⊗ in this and the succeeding diagrams designates the bridling or tie point.

## CUBIC KITE (See color photo insert)

By changing the disposition of these regular six-sided units, as the diagrams suggest, you can create an empty space in the middle.

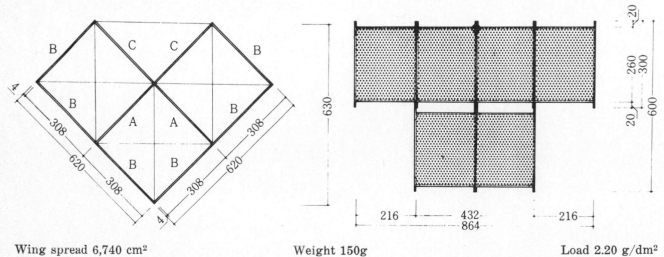

Wing spread 6,740 cm²          Weight 150g          Load 2.20 g/dm²

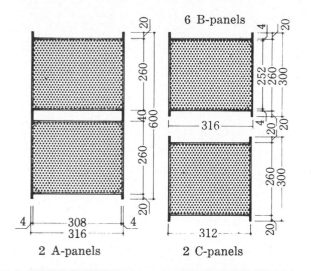

6 B-panels

2 A-panels

2 C-panels

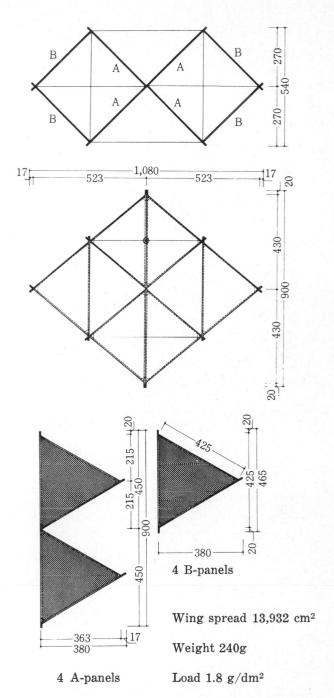

4 A-panels

4 B-panels

Wing spread 13,932 cm²

Weight 240g

Load 1.8 g/dm²

## DIAMOND KITE

Built according to truss construction principles, this kite can stand up to a rather strong wind. High among the clouds, it looks like a jewel inlaid with velvet cloth.

# SIX-WINGED KITE

The special effect of this creation is produced by the addition of six round-tipped insect-like wings.

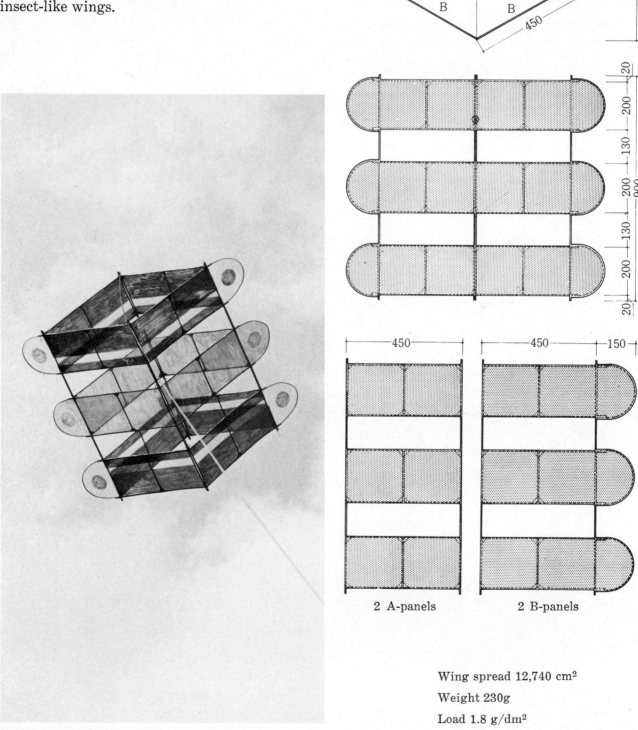

2 A-panels          2 B-panels

Wing spread 12,740 cm²

Weight 230g

Load 1.8 g/dm²

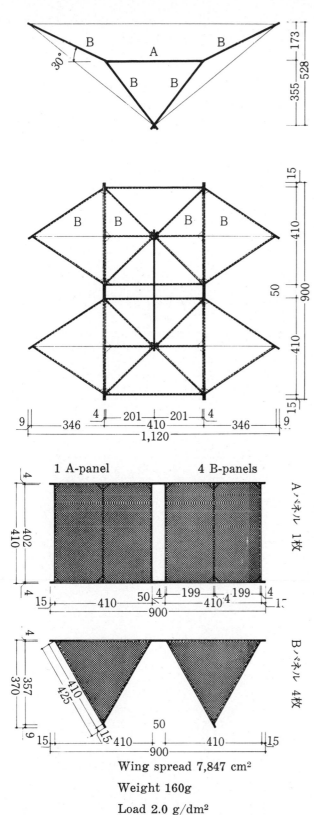

1 A-panel      4 B-panels

Aパネル　1枚

Bパネル　4枚

Wing spread 7,847 cm²

Weight 160g

Load 2.0 g/dm²

## KUSHIGATA (SKEWER-SHAPE) KITE

This kite, shaped like the ideograph for skewer, calls to mind a wild duck taking flight. It is very contemporary looking with its red and blue striped pattern.

# TIGER KITE (See color photo insert)

The tiger rolls its red tongue in a gesture of strength and good humor. Two basic box forms are linked by an additional unit.

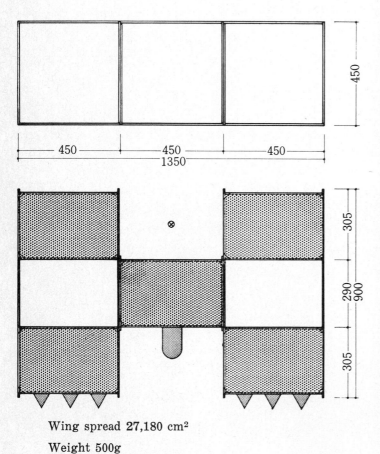

Wing spread **27,180 cm²**

Weight **500g**

Load **1.83 g/dm²**

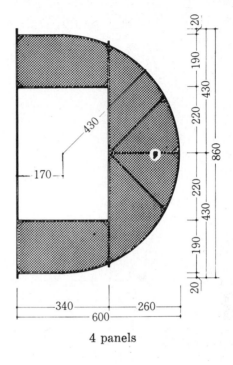

4 panels

Wing spread 11,284 cm²
Weight 280g
Load 2.4 g/dm²

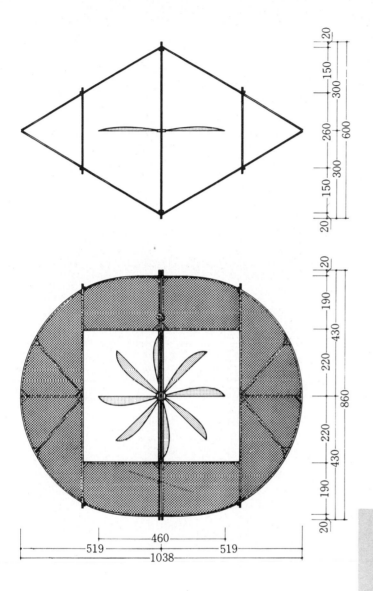

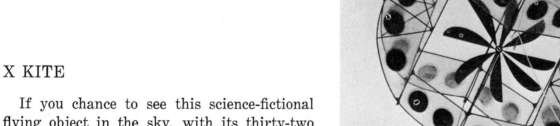

## X KITE

If you chance to see this science-fictional flying object in the sky, with its thirty-two dots swimming around a revolving body, you may well feel that you are in the presence of latent energy seeking to be released.

## MACH 9 KITE (See color photo insert)

This multicellular rhomboid appears to be moving even as it hovers quietly in the air. Take four of these, put them together, and what have you got? Answer: the three-dimensional monster kite to the right, testimony to man's ever-expanding consciousness.

Wing spread 22,896 cm²

Weight 500g

Load 2.1 g/dm²

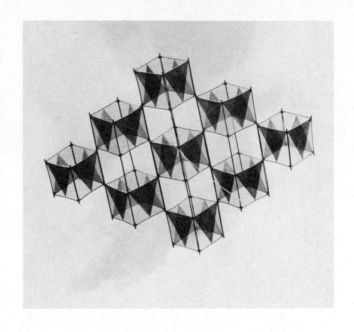

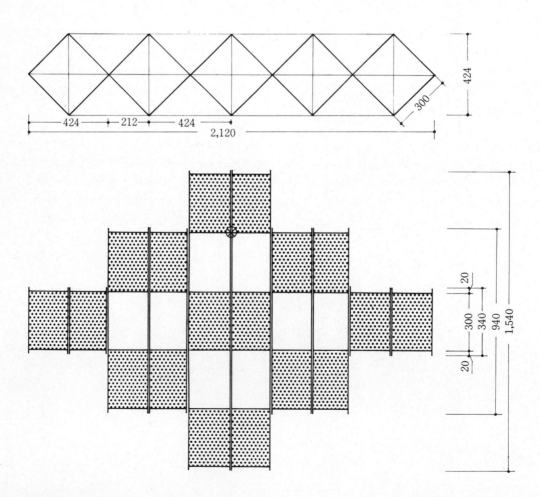

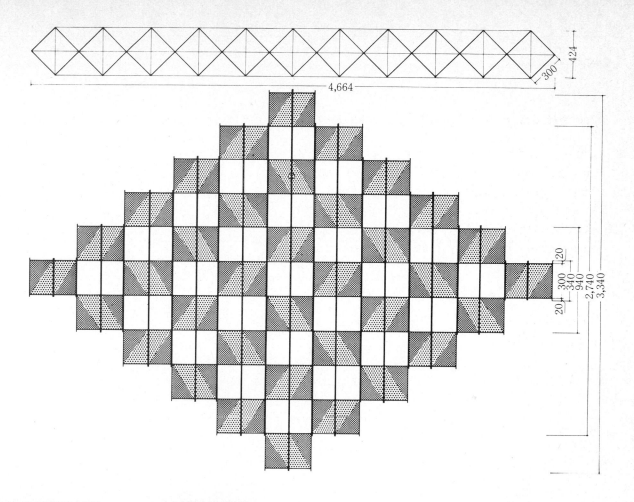

## THREE-DIMENSIONAL (SOARING) GIANT KITE

This 144-unit giant structure is an attempt to expand the number of basic box kites that can be successfully joined and flown together. A great deal of care is required to assemble and handle this kite. But to see it soaring in the sky is to witness the birth of a new type of space design. (See book jacket cover illustration.)

The photograph shows the giant kite turned on its head with its bridle legs hanging out. The numerous bridles are crucial to the construction; they give the kite added strength to resist the wind.

Wing spread 91,584 cm²

Weight 200g

Load 2.1 g/dm²

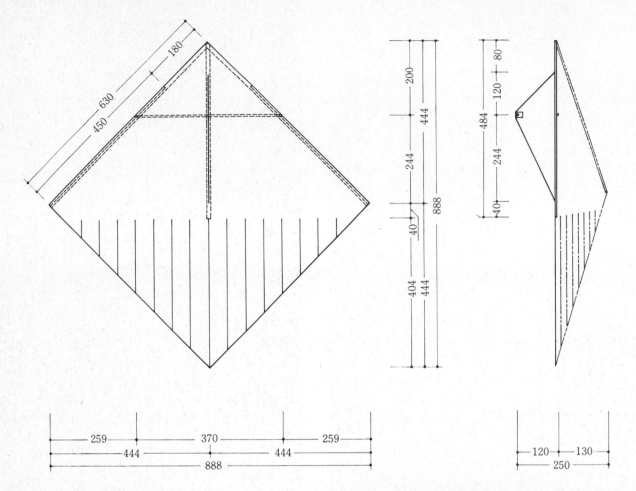

Wing spread 1,985 cm²

Weight 30g

Load 1.5 g/dm²

## SPACE MEDUSA
(See color photo insert)

Kites are not only seekers of new spatial forms; they can also be storytellers in the heavens. Listen for the pitter-patter of footsteps as these visitors from outer space tiptoe across the sky.

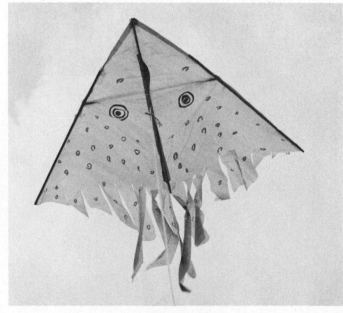

## ONE-EYE

This contemporary psychedelic ghoul sports a fluorescent green and pink design on a silver background.

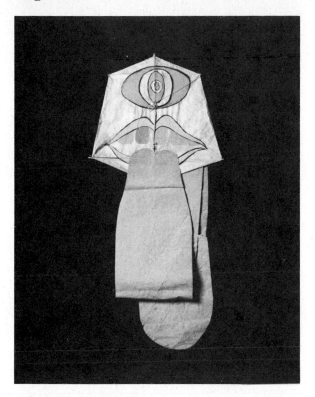

## THUNDER GOD

This awe-inspiring kite is painted with wax using batik techniques. The light shines through the wax impression.

## DRESSING UP

A very pretty flight by an elegant kite, the creation of a young schoolgirl.

## GORILLA

This powerful-looking beast may have weak arms and legs, but it flies well thanks to the strongly developed curvature of its torso.

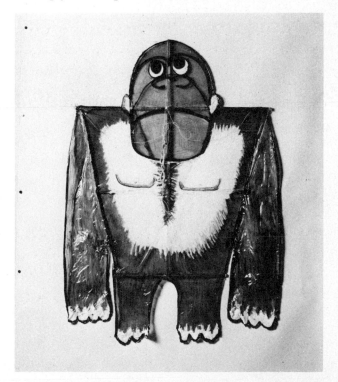

# 5
# Kites Around the World: Good Design

From their birthplace in China, kites spread to one country after another, evolving in distinct and original ways all over the world. Today, the countless progeny of these early pioneer kites continue the traditions of their ancestors, at the same time reflecting the distinctive national character of their respective homelands.

The variety of generic Chinese terms for kites have different etymological associations with birds, sky, air, etc., the most common being *fon tien* (wind harp). As we see in the following list of names, different cultures evolved their own generic term for kites with various associations between the kite and the sky:

*Kite* (English derivation from the name for falcon, a bird of prey)
*Drachen* (German for dragon)
*Cerf-volant* (French for stag-beetle)
*Cometa* (Spanish for comet)
*Papagaio* (Portuguese for parrot)
*Aquilone* (Italian for north wind)
*Lajang* or *Laiang* (Indonesian for flying object)
*Sarungal* (Indo-Ceylonese for paper-flying object)
*Gai-deu* (Vietnamese for bird)
*Waw* (Thai generic term for kite): *Chula* ("bird," meaning male kite); *Pakpao* ("fish," meaning female kite)
*Yan* (Korean for hawk, corresponding to the Japanese *tombi*)

Let's take a look at the distinguishing characteristics of some of these varied kites, those that reflect a particular cultural heritage as well as those that are noteworthy for their distinctive structural forms. In each case, we shall be concerned with those features that may be considered aspects of superior design.

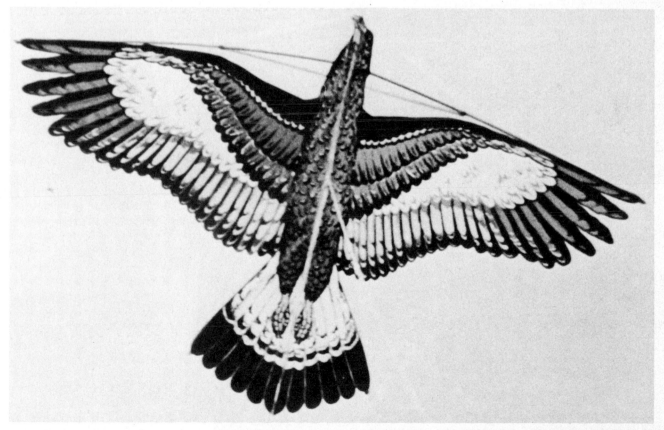

This peacock kite from Thailand, which vies with Japan as the land of kites, trails its cerulean blue crepe-paper tail gracefully through the heavens.

A white-tailed eagle kite from Germany. This high-flying bird, painted on transparent vinyl, has been known to fool live hawks into thinking their domains have been threatened, prompting full-scale attacks on the unsuspecting kite.

We may also take note of the appearance in recent years (in the United States and Germany, for the most part) of a significant number of kites representing revolutionary developments in kite design. Designed above all with a view to high-efficiency aerodynamic performance, these may be divided into seven types: delta wing, flexible, parasail, Parafoil, inflatable, cubic, and revolving wing.

## RAINCOAT KITE (Japan)

This kite proves that even the most familiar, everyday objects can take to the skies. This kite is made from a cheap plastic raincoat. It operates on the same principle as the *gunya-gunya* kite. When the rays of the sun penetrate this traditional Japanese design, one is treated to an extraordinary visual delight.

To make your own raincoat kite, just attach two long 10mm-thick cypress strips to the front of a plastic raincoat at the points indicated in the diagram. Experiment until you've determined the best place to attach the bridle. The hood may be left attached; it will inflate in flight and function as a brake, preventing the kite from going beyond its apex and taking a nose dive. The kite was designed by the author.

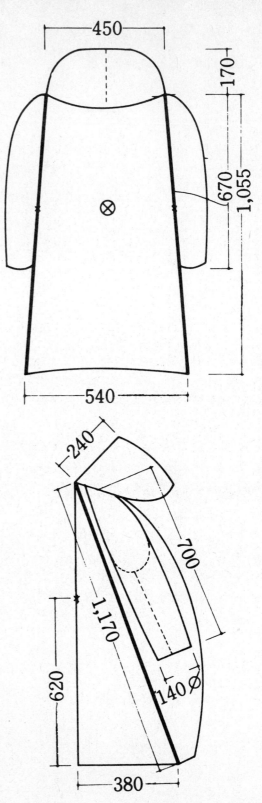

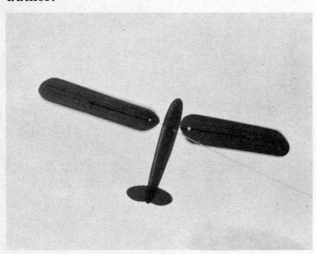

This turbomach kite from Germany uses the same rotational principle that allows a baseball player to throw a curve ball. A new design of kite, it also comes in a dragonfly model with rolling eyes.

## PUFFER KITE (United States)
### (See color photo insert)

This is a modern-day vinyl balloon kite that retains the proportions of the traditional Western bow kite. A single bridle suffices for this lightweight flier.

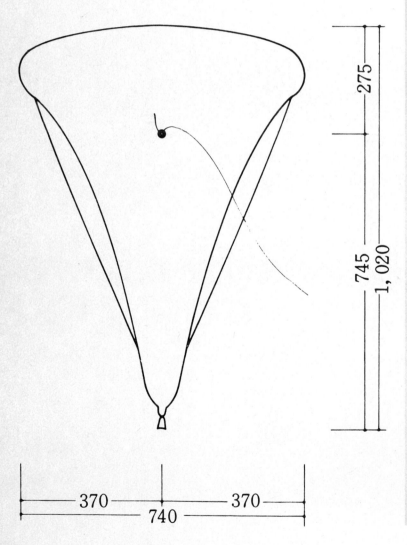

275

745

1,020

370 370

740

# JALBERT PARAFOIL (United States)

A true innovation in design and the use of basic materials, the Jalbert Parafoil displays a high level of aerodynamic prowess. Improving on its predecessor, the flexible kite, the Parafoil has completely eliminated the need for a rigid skeleton, replacing it with a series of wind-inflated cylindrically shaped units. It is the air itself, entering the structure from the top, that assumes the usual functions of the frame. The Parafoil also features "flutter" valves of cloth inside the air intake, which adhere to the inner surface and prevent air from escaping when the pressure is inadequate. Flaps of cloth attached to the kite center and bottom reinforce stability. The Parafoil inflates to a size of 120cm × 160cm when flying but deflates to a compact 200cm.[3] The tremendous efficiency of design makes it a straight and steady flier with adequate wind and space. In strong winds, it will fly straight overhead. Through the combination of horizontal units, it

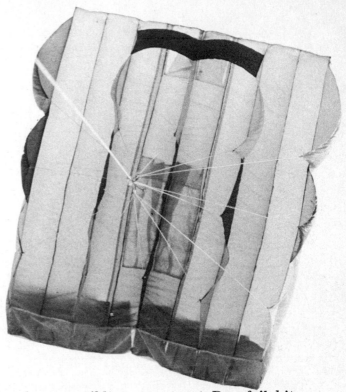

has been possible to construct Parafoil kites capable of lifting objects weighing as much as 80kg.

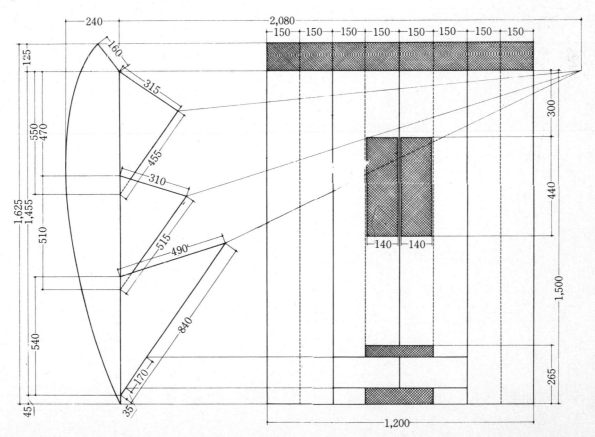

## GRECIAN KITE (Greece)

Picture this perfectly geometrical hexagonal kite being flown by children atop a small rise with the Parthenon in the background. It is made quintessentially Greek, moreover, by the tassel design fringing its six-sided rim.

To construct it, cross three 700mm-long strips of 4mm square cypress and tie them together at the center. Tape a hexagonally cut piece of polyethylene film (radius 300mm) to the bottom, using vinyl tape. Stretch a string around the border edges and attach thin tassels cut from polyethylene tape. Use a three-legged bridle, setting the tie point in the mid-

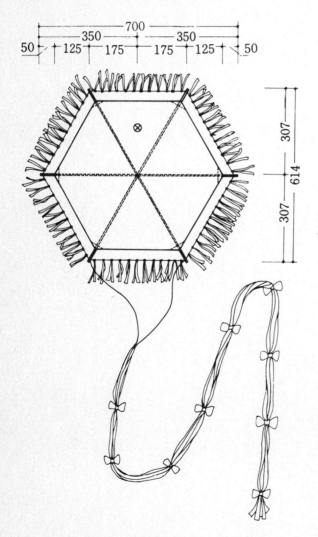

dle of the uppermost triangle, as indicated in the diagram. Fly your Grecian kite as it is; bowing is unnecessary.

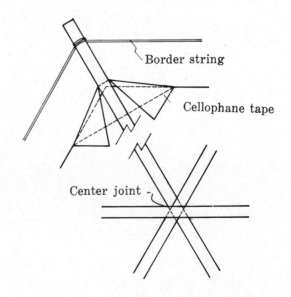

## CENTIPEDE KITE (China)
(See color photo insert)

Chinese kites display a superb technical ingenuity and as fine an attention to detail as one is likely to find anywhere in the world. This most original centipede kite is highly efficient. Weighing only 750g, it can easily be transported by hand once the line and discs have been arranged in a pile. It is a vivid example of how splendidly the ancient Chinese had already resolved the aerodynamic complexities of equilibrium. The centipede's windpowered rolling eyes are functional as well as decorative—they measure wind speed.

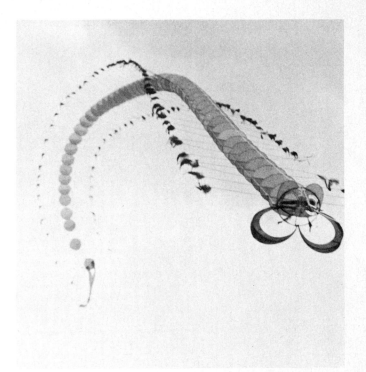

## CONSTRUCTION

1. You may have anywhere from eight to fifty round discs, each about 23cm in diameter made from bamboo slats. While it is best to use slats split from a single shoot of bamboo, purchased ones will do.

2. Bamboo slats are also used for the horizontal rods, which should each be about 120cm long. If they are too short, the kite will be unstable and difficult to fly. Tie each rod to a disc front; then cover the disc with paper or vinyl film. Choose materials which make the structure as light as possible.

3. Attach about five bird feathers to each rod end. Tie the discs together with string in three places, at the tops and sides.

4. Devise your own three-dimensional head with eyes that roll, and attach it with string to the first disc.

5. The bridle lines should be attached to the head at points A (top) and B₁ and B₂ (left and right sides). Set the tie point so that the upper leg (A) is shorter, forming a 40° angle with the side legs.

Attaching two meter-long cloth tails (5cm wide) beneath the last disc will give added balance to the rear section.

When launching this somewhat uncoordinated winged reptile, it is best to first lay it out flat on the ground, accurately oriented in

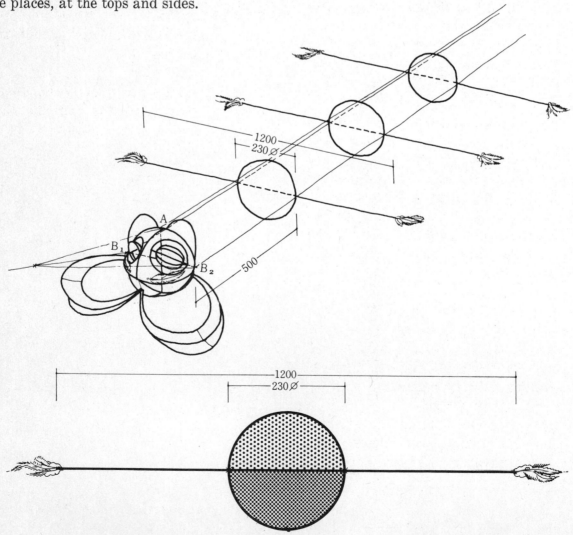

the direction of the wind. Then, pulling the flying line over your shoulder, run about 5 or 6 meters with it. The head should lift up, dragging the rest of the body behind it slowly, as if it were swimming. The long rods protruding from the sides act to lower the center of gravity, and thus help maintain horizontal equilibrium much as the poles used by circus tightrope walkers aid their balance. When the wind hits the feather tips, it creates weight on the end of the rod (in the form of resistance to the force of the wind), thus maintaining the kite in equilibrium.

## COBRA KITE (Thailand)
(See color photo insert)

Thailand, no less than Japan, boasts a prodigious variety of kites and is known as the "land of kites." This easy-to-build cobra kite, which can be made in both large and small sizes, owes its lifelike serpentine body motion to the skillful exploitation of the *dis*equilibrium it suffers due to lapses in wind strength.

### CONSTRUCTION
1. Assemble three bamboo slats into the shape of the letter *I*. Tie the upper crosspiece, which should be a bit thicker in the middle, to the top of the vertical shaft, and attach the lower crosspiece to the bottom, making sure that they are perpendicular.

2. Now connect the upper crosspiece to the lower one by tying strings to both ends. Bend the upper slat into an arc reaching a third of the way down from the top to form the head of the cobra. Cover it with paper or vinyl.

3. Use crepe paper for the tail, and attach it to the lower end of the frame. Make it 5m long and taper it from a width of 16cm.

4. Draw your cobra's features on the head, and decorate the tail.

5. Set the bridling point at 11cm or a third of the way down from the kite top. Additional bowing is unnecessary; the cobra flies well with its head flat.

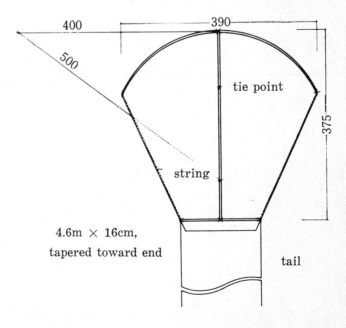

# KOREAN KITE (Korea)

This fighter kite has a central vent that functions in much the same way as an airplane's flap wings, regulating the airflow by allowing excess air pressure on the kite's surface to pass through.

This particular kite has been designed small by Takeshi Nishibayashi. Lacking a central horizontal spar, it is an example of lightweight precision, flying well in a gentle breeze. With a flying line of thin silk, and a reel, this kite has been known to ride an updraft straight up as high as 1,300m.

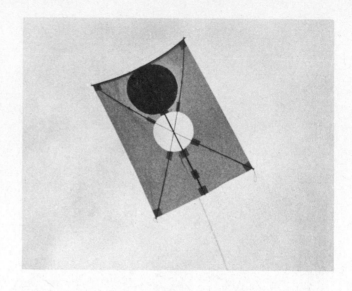

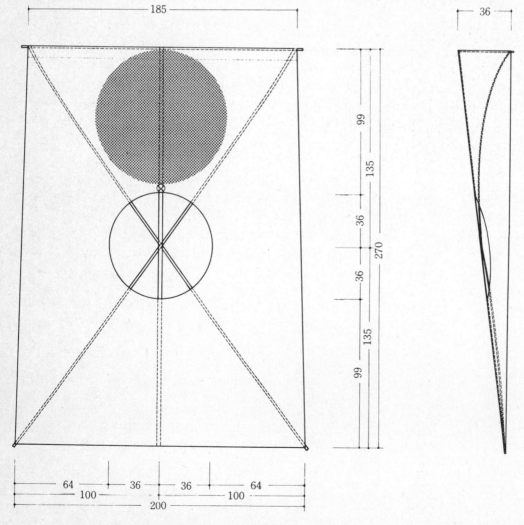

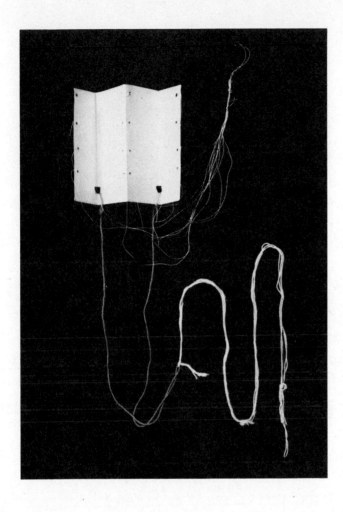

## FOLDING KITE (Japan)

This kite is native to the remote solitary island of Aogashima (south of Hachijo Island). The children of the island make it by folding pieces of notebook paper into four sections, making three rows of four holes each with an incense stick, and passing twelve lengths of thread through the twelve holes. This is enough to give the thin paper surface complete support. The folded surfaces replace the nonexistent frame. Do not underestimate this simple structure. Its functionality is on a par with the most elaborate three-dimensional kites, and even ultramodern frameless creations such as the Jalbert Parafoil (p. 119).

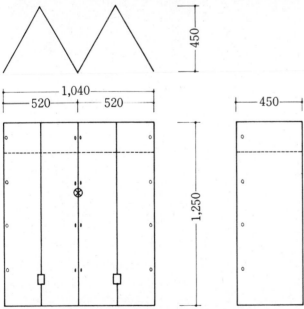

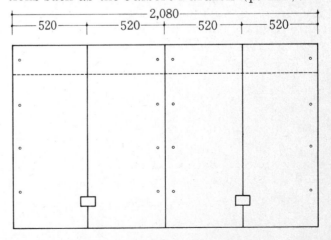

## OWL KITE (Japan)

This owl kite, popular with children in Tokyo's Koganei district in the late 1920s, is related to the folding kite. The bridle has four legs, one each on the top left and right ends and two on the center fold. Small strips of paper are pasted under the string holes to keep the bridle line ends in place.

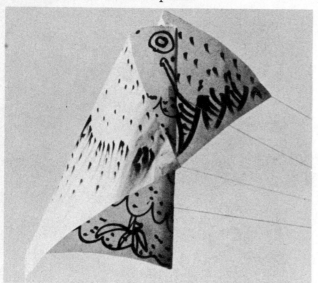

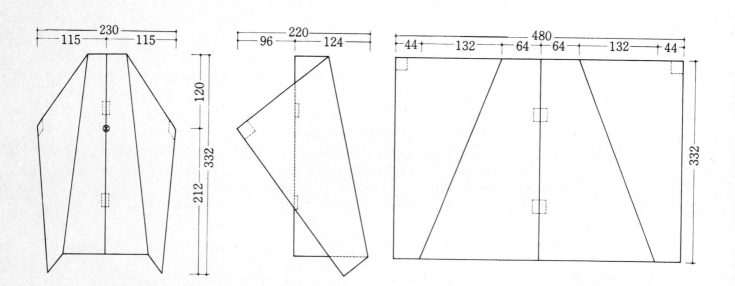

## BOW KITE (United States)

The most representative type of Western kite, the bow consists of two crossed spars, the horizontal one curved into an arc, and a tail of ribbon reminiscent of Benjamin Franklin's kite. The version shown here is an American collapsible type. In England, cotton cloth is often used, and the front may feature a triangular keel for stability.

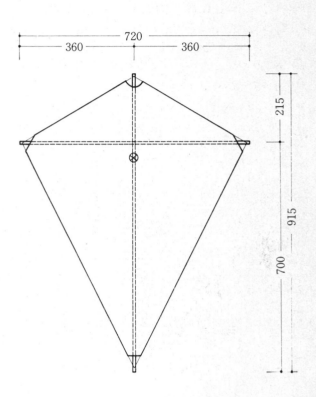

## NAGASAKI HATA (Japan)

A friend of mine who tried to buy a kite in Nagasaki came dangerously close to being escorted to the fish market. In Tokyo, the query "Where can I buy a kite?" can be ambiguous, as the usual word for kite, *tako*, has the same pronunciation as the word for octopus. In Nagasaki, *tako* refers exclusively to this favorite Japanese delicacy. What if you still want to buy a kite, then? The word you must use in the Nagasaki region is *hata*, which admittedly could give rise to a different kind of confusion; it is also the usual word for flag. Indeed, the term does undoubtedly derive from the resemblance of the local variety of kite to a four-sided flag.

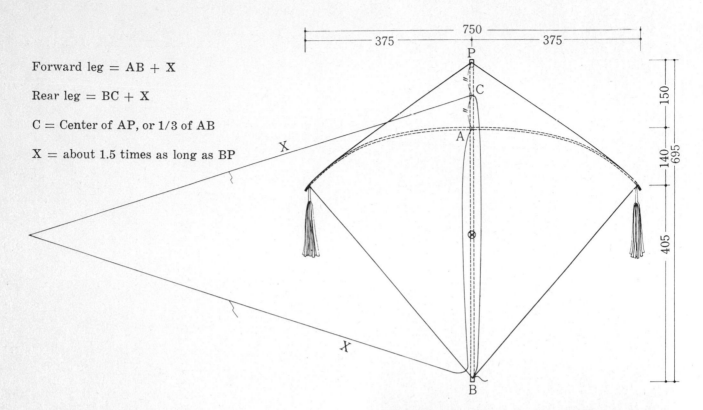

Forward leg = AB + X

Rear leg = BC + X

C = Center of AP, or 1/3 of AB

X = about 1.5 times as long as BP

Every April in Nagasaki, a time and a place are decided upon for the annual kite-fighting festival. *Hata* fighters are flown with a special hemp line (*yoma*) distinguished by its menacing coating of ground glass paste (*bidoro*). The lines of the competing kites swish at each other in the sky until one goes down to defeat.

The *hata* kite is made of two thin strips of long-jointed bamboo, a vertical spine and a horizontal bow tapered toward the ends. Strings are attached to keep the bow in place. For stabilization, the bow also has paper tassels (*hyu*) attached to its extremities. This simple, functional form is supported by a two-legged bridle attached to the spine. Bending naturally in response to wind variations, the *hata* is highly maneuverable.

Nagasaki *hata* kites feature two types of decoration. The *moyo*, or "pattern," type involves the cutting and pasting of different colored papers to produce a specific design. The *shima*, or "striped," type consists of as many

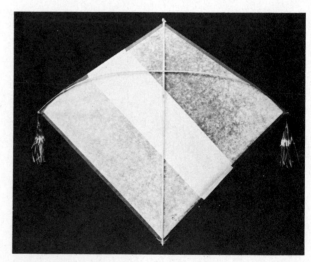

as 120 geometric variations of the traditional red, white, and blue stripes.

While it is extremely simple in design and structure, the proper construction of the *hata* still requires considerable skill and a delicate touch. It is, moreover, worthy of the best flat kite design, if its dynamic performance in the air is any indication.

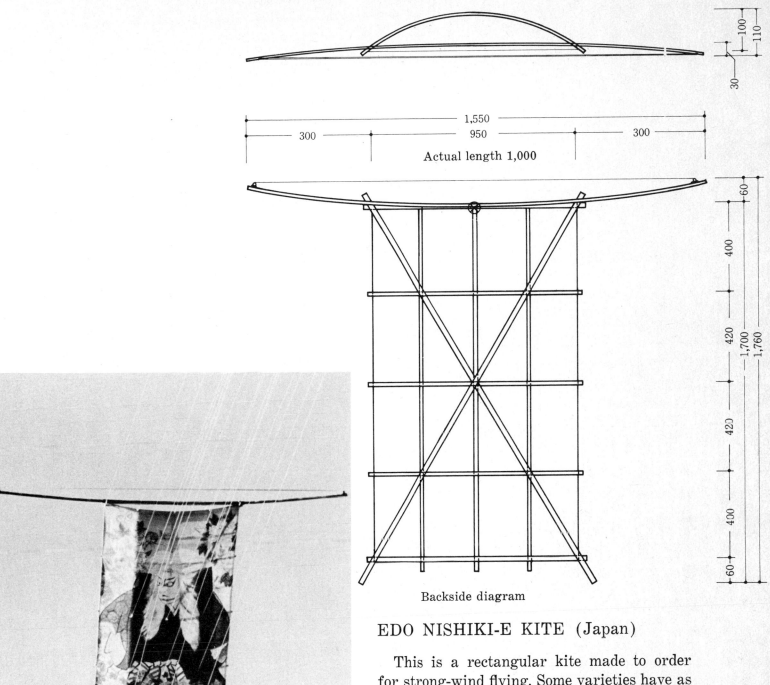

1,550
300
950
300
Actual length 1,000

100
110
30

60
60
400
420
420
400
60
1,700
1,760

Backside diagram

## EDO NISHIKI-E KITE (Japan)

This is a rectangular kite made to order for strong-wind flying. Some varieties have as many as seventeen 36m-long bridles. For easier handling, these lines may be attached to an unbreakable leather grid (photo, p. 131). The collapsible model diagrammed here was designed by Katsuhisa Ota. The symmetrical frame is constructed with unusual precision. The sections that are to form the nodes are heated and flattened.

Edo kite with painting depicting scene from the Kabuki play *Kagami jishi* (The Dancing Lion)

There are still a few Edo kite masters to be found in Tokyo today. One of them is Naotaka Fujita, an expert paperhanger, who covers his kites with fabric-reinforced *washi* paper. The kite pictured here, with hummer attached, weighs 2,500g and has a wing load of $15g/cm^2$, making it a highly wind-resistant flier.

Naotaka Fujita attaching a hummer to his Edo kite

Flowing, silver-white shrouds stream through the sky

At Shibamata along the Edogawa River, where the wind is so fierce a man has trouble standing firm, the lone kite-maker assembles his creation, drives a stake into the ground, and attaches a thick hemp flying line to it. Now he can fly his kite single-handedly. With over 30kg of pull, this kite is about the largest a man dare fly by himself, making it what one could call a "one-man giant kite."

Katsuhisa Ota maneuvering his bridle lines with the aid of a grid

# Appendixes

## Kite Dimensions and Calculations

The terms "heavy" and "light" as I have used them refer not just to the weight of the kite, but to its weight relative to the wing surface area or wing spread, which is the sum of the areas of the individual wing surfaces. This will affect the way in which the kite will react to the different winds it encounters. Wing load is the weight of the kite per 1dm² (100 cm²) of wing spread, and is calculated in this manner:

$$\frac{\text{wing load}}{(\text{g/dm}^2)} = \frac{\text{kite weight (g)}}{\text{wing spread (cm}^2)} \times 100$$

The box kite we built first, diagrammed on page 69, weighs 160g. Its wing load and spread are determined thus:

Varying the relative dimensions of your kite will affect its strength, resistance, and stability. The following chart compares the performances of three types of three-dimensional kites, all having the same size frame but differing in terms of wing spread. Kite A has narrow wings, making it an effective glider-like flier with just a thin string as a flying line. Kite B has a larger wing spread than A, and can fly well even in a relatively light breeze. While Kite C's large wing spread makes it a good light-breeze flier, there is a risk of its being damaged if it strikes a strong wind at high altitude.

$$\text{wing spread} = 65.4 \text{ (cm)} \times 28.0 \text{ (cm)} \times 4 = 7324.8 \text{ (cm}^2)$$
$$\text{wing load} = \frac{160\text{g}}{7324.8 \text{ cm}^2} \times 100 = 2.1843\text{g/dm}^2$$

| | 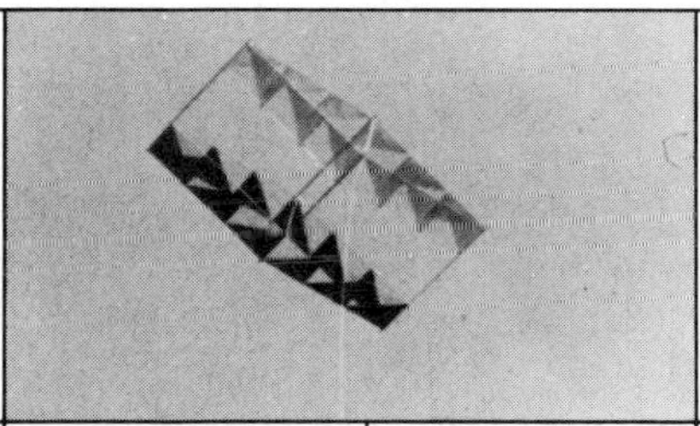 | | 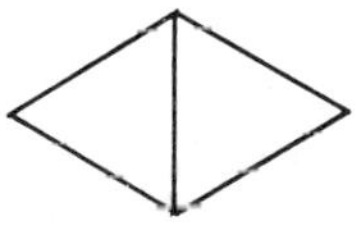 Light breeze (leaves rustle); wind speed 4–7 mph | 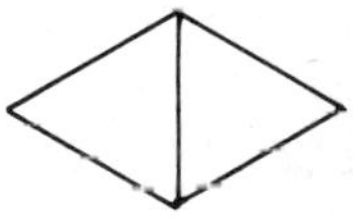 Gentle breeze (small twigs move); wind speed 8–12 mph | 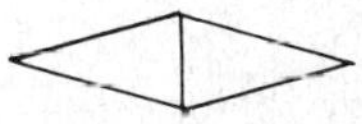 Dihedral angle reduced by 1/2 at 8–12 mph wind speed |
|---|---|---|---|---|---|
| | KITE A Wing span=1/4 of total length Weight: 303g Wing area: 12,096cm² Load: 2.727g/dm² | Line pull | About 300g | About 600g | About 750g |
| | | Stability | Maintains equilibrium, but will sink at lower wind speed | Maintains equilibrium | Wobbles |
| | | Strength (flexion of materials) | 0–2.5cm | 2.5–5cm | 2.5–5cm |
| | KITE B Wing span=1/3 of total length Weight: 350g Wing area: 16,128cm² Load: 2.23g/dm² | Line pull | About 650g | About 1,300g | About 1,625g |
| | | Stability | Maintains equilibrium | Maintains equilibrium | Wobbling intensifies |
| | | Strength (flexion of materials) | 1.2–3.7cm | 3.7–7.5cm | 3.7–7.5cm |
| | KITE C Wing span=3/7 of total length Weight: 380g Wing area: 20,880cm² Load: 1.82g/dm² | Line pull | About 1,000g | About 2,000g | About 2,500g |
| | | Stability | Maintains equilibrium | In any stronger wind than this, kite risks destruction | Stability worsens; kite risks plunging in direction of its tilt |
| | | Strength (flexion of materials) | 2.5–5cm | 5–10cm | 5–10cm |

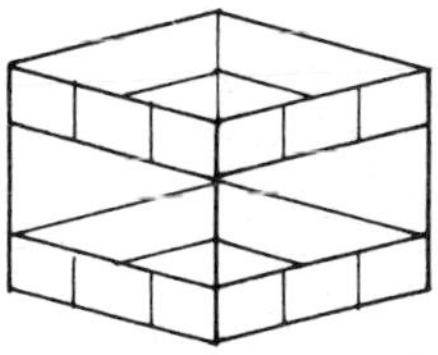

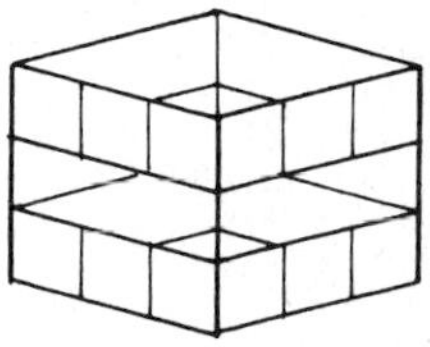

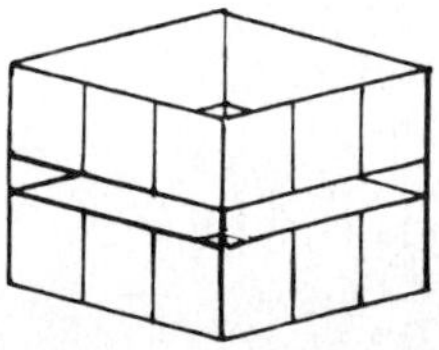

| | angle | 10° | 20° | 30° | 40° | 45° | 50° | 60° | 70° | 80° | 90° |
|---|---|---|---|---|---|---|---|---|---|---|---|
| 100m | height | 17.36 | 34.2 | 50 | 64.28 | 70.71 | 76.6 | 86.6 | 93.97 | 98.48 | 100 |
| | distance | 98.48 | 93.97 | 86.6 | 76.6 | | 64.28 | 50 | 34.2 | 17.36 | |
| 200m | height | 34.72 | 68.4 | 100 | 128.56 | 141.42 | 153.2 | 173.2 | 187.94 | 196.96 | 200 |
| | distance | 196.96 | 187.94 | 173.2 | 153.2 | | 128.56 | 100 | 68.4 | 34.72 | |
| 300m | height | 52.08 | 102.6 | 150 | 192.84 | 212.13 | 229.8 | 259.8 | 281.91 | 295.44 | 300 |
| | distance | 295.44 | 281.91 | 259.8 | 229.8 | | 192.84 | 150 | 102.6 | 52.08 | |
| 400m | height | 69.44 | 136.8 | 200 | 257.12 | 282.84 | 306.4 | 346.4 | 375.88 | 393.92 | 400 |
| | distance | 393.92 | 375.88 | 346.4 | 306.4 | | 257.12 | 200 | 136.8 | 69.44 | |
| 500m | height | 86.8 | 171 | 250 | 321.4 | 353.55 | 383 | 433 | 469.85 | 492.4 | 500 |
| | distance | 492.40 | 469.85 | 433 | 383 | | 321.4 | 250 | 171 | 86.8 | |
| 600m | height | 104.16 | 205.2 | 300 | 385.68 | 424.26 | 459.6 | 519.6 | 563.82 | 590.88 | 600 |
| | distance | 590.88 | 563.82 | 519.6 | 159.6 | | 385.68 | 300 | 205.2 | 104.16 | |
| 700m | height | 121.52 | 239.4 | 350 | 449.96 | 494.97 | 536.2 | 606.2 | 657.79 | 689.36 | 700 |
| | distance | 689.36 | 657.79 | 606.2 | 536.2 | | 449.96 | 350 | 239.4 | 121.52 | |
| 800m | height | 138.88 | 273.6 | 400 | 514.24 | 565.68 | 612.8 | 692.8 | 751.76 | 787.84 | 800 |
| | distance | 787.84 | 751.76 | 692.8 | 612.8 | | 514.24 | 400 | 273.6 | 138.88 | |
| 900m | height | 156.24 | 307.8 | 450 | 578.52 | 636.39 | 689.4 | 779.4 | 845.73 | 886.32 | 900 |
| | distance | 886.32 | 845.73 | 779.4 | 689.4 | | 578.52 | 450 | 307.8 | 156.24 | |
| 1000m | height | 173.6 | 342 | 500 | 642.8 | 707.1 | 766 | 866 | 939.7 | 984.8 | 1000 |
| | distance | 984.8 | 939.7 | 866 | 766 | | 642.8 | 500 | 342 | 173.6 | |
| 1500m | height | 260.4 | 513 | 750 | 964.2 | 1060.65 | 1149 | 1299 | 1409.55 | 1477.2 | 1500 |
| | distance | 1477.2 | 1409.55 | 1299 | 1149 | | 964.2 | 750 | 513 | 260.4 | |
| 2000m | height | 347.2 | 684 | 1000 | 1285.6 | 1414.2 | 1532 | 1732 | 1879.4 | 1969.6 | 2000 |
| | distance | 1969.6 | 1879.4 | 1732 | 1532 | | 1285.6 | 1000 | 684 | 347.2 | |
| 3000m | height | 520.8 | 1026 | 1500 | 1928.4 | 2121.3 | 2298 | 2598 | 2819.1 | 2954.4 | 3000 |
| | distance | 2954.4 | 2819.1 | 2598 | 2298 | | 1928.4 | 1500 | 1026 | 520.8 | |

# Wind Chart

Beaufort's scale was devised about 1805 by Admiral Francis Beaufort of the British navy to help sailors gauge wind conditions at sea. The scale ranges from 0 (calm) through various breezes, gales, and storms to 12 (hurricane). Light, steady winds of eight to fifteen miles per hour are ideal for the average kite, though delicate kites with a great deal of lift will respond to lighter breezes. Wind speeds of up to twenty miles per hour are generally safe for sturdy kites with good stability and strong lines, but only exceptionally strong kites should be flown in winds of over twenty-four miles per hour, and even then the flyer risks losing the kite. As a tree-smashing gale is usually an effective deterrent to even the most enthusiastic of kite flyers, only a partial Beaufort's scale, modified for land use, is shown here.

Edo *nishiki-e* kite-maker Teizo Hashimoto in his workshop

| Beaufort # | Term | mph | Effects on land |
|---|---|---|---|
| 0 | Calm | 0 | Smoke rises vertically |
| 1 | Light air | 1–3 | Smoke drift shows wind direction but vanes don't move |
| 2 | Light breeze | 4–7 | Wind felt on face; leaves rustle; vanes turn |
| 3 | Gentle breeze | 8–12 | Leaves and small twigs in constant motion; light flags extend |
| 4 | Moderate breeze | 13–18 | Dust and loose paper raised; small branches move |
| 5 | Fresh breeze | 19–24 | Small trees in leaf begin to sway |
| 6 | Strong breeze | 25–31 | Large branches move; telegraph wires whistle |

# Weight and Measurement Chart

All weights and measurements in this book are expressed in metric form. However, for the convenience of the American reader, some common equivalents and conversions to U.S. units are listed below.

1 kilogram = 10 hectograms = 100 dekagrams = 1000 grams

1 kilometer = 1000 meters

1 meter = 10 decimeters = 100 centimeters = 1000 millimeters

| | | |
|---|---|---|
| 1 gram = 0.035 ounce | 1 kilogram = | 2.2 pounds |
| 2 grams = 0.075 ounce | 2 kilograms = | 4.4 pounds |
| 3 grams = 0.106 ounce | 3 kilograms = | 6.6 pounds |
| 4 grams = 0.141 ounce | 4 kilograms = | 8.8 pounds |
| 5 grams = 0.177 ounce | 5 kilograms = | 11.0 pounds |
| 10 grams = 0.353 ounce | 10 kilograms = | 22.0 pounds |
| 50 grams = 1.765 ounces | 50 kilograms = | 110.2 pounds |
| 100 grams = 3.527 ounces | 100 kilograms = | 220.4 pounds |

1 g/cm$^2$ = 0.2275 oz/in$^2$

1 cm$^3$ = 0.061 in$^3$      1 millimeter = 0.039 inches

1 meter = 39.37 inches = 3.28 feet = 1.09 yards

2 meters = 78.74 inches = 6.56 feet = 2.19 yards

3 meters = 118.11 inches = 9.84 feet = 3.28 yards

4 meters = 157.48 inches = 13.12 feet = 4.37 yards

5 meters = 196.85 inches = 16.40 feet = 5.47 yards

10 meters = 393.70 inches = 32.81 feet = 10.94 yards

50 meters = 1968.51 inches = 164.04 feet = 54.68 yards

100 meters = 3937.01 inches = 328.08 feet = 109.36 yards

1 centimeter = 0.39 inch

2 centimeters = 0.79 inch

3 centimeters = 1.18 inches

4 centimeters = 1.57 inches

5 centimeters = 1.97 inches

10 centimeters = 3.94 inches

50 centimeters = 19.69 inches

100 centimeters = 39.37 inches

# A Glossary of Selected Japanese Kite Terms

*bekako*   funny face

*buka*   refers to sound certain kites make when rising into the air

*daruma*   Buddhist monk

*donko*   fishlike

*emmadojin*   King of Hades

*fon tien*   wind harp; Chinese generic term for kite

*fugo*   blowfish

*fukusuke*   lucky gnome

*gunya-gunya*   limp or flabby

*hakkaku*   octagonal

*hannya*   type of demon kite

*hata*   flag; popular generic term for kite

*hyottoko*   droll fellow

*ika*   squid

*iwaidako*   celebrational kite

*koma*   spinning top

*kushigata*   skewer shape

*makiika*   rolled squid

*managu*   eye

*mimimagari*   curved ear

*nishiki-e*   brocade picture; with *tako*, color print kite

*oniyozu*   demon kite

*rokkaku*   hexagonal

*semi*   cicada

*shima*   stripe

*sode*   sleeve of kimono

*tako*   octopus; common generic term for kite

*tombi*   hawk

*unari*   hummers; devices that travel up and down the flying line of an airborne kite, making weird noises as they go

*yakko*   footman

*yokanbei*   variation of the *yakko* kite

*yozu*   suggests demonic force

# The Japan Kite Association (Nihon no Tako no Kai)

The activities of the association include regular meetings, kite-flying outings, kite-study groups, and publication of a club bulletin twice a year. All kite enthusiasts are welcome to become members free of charge. Current membership stands at 1500 members. The address to write to is Nihon no Tako no Kai, c/o Mr. Shingo Modegi, The Taimeiken Restaurant, 1-12-10 Nihonbashi, Chuo-ku, Tokyo 103.

## KITE FESTIVALS

The following is a selected list of kite festivals in the United States and Canada. At this writing, approximately 45 such events are held regularly each year. Many others are conducted on a more casual basis. As with any index captured at one moment in time, new festivals are continually becoming established, while some old events may be fading away. A comprehensive quarterly update of kite events appears on the calendar page of *Kite Lines*, journal of the American Kitefliers Association.

At this time, the American Kitefliers Association does not endorse, sanction, or sponsor any kite event directly but only serves as a clearinghouse of information about them. Kite festivals are organized in a multitude of ways and are a reflection of the communities they serve and the different views of the individual organizers behind them. For example, some festivals limit entries to "home-made" kites, some do not. Age classes are kept separate at most meets. Usually registration is free, but a few events charge entry fees. The events are variously christened as *festivals, flies, competitions, tournaments, contests,* etc. The nomenclature is not exact or very important, for most events are competitive in some fashion (though some are more so than others and a few are non-competitive).

Only two standards have been applied to inclusion of listings in the following selection: one is that an event must have been held for at least two years; the other is that it must be open to adults and therefore, presumably, of serious interest. Such variables as size of crowd, quality of kites, value of prizes, character of setting and organization, etc., while important, are very slippery as standards and often inflated by promoters. Sometimes it is the "small" gathering that will produce the best kites, keenest judging, and happiest atmosphere—unknown to the rest of the world. This list makes no judgments and no promises. The reader is invited to discover his or her own favorite occasions for sharing and glorying in kiteflying.

The list is arranged in order of states. The long-established festivals are usually, but not necessarily, larger and better organized. Festival ages given are for the year 1978.

## Alabama

First March Saturday: MARS Kite Derby, Marshall Space Flight Center (for employees and families), Huntsville, AL. *Sponsor*: M.S.F.C. Athletic, Recreational and Social Exchange. *Contact*: Richard A. Love, 2002 Giles Drive, N.E., Huntsville, AL 35811. 10th annual in 1978.

## California

First March Saturday: Plaza Camino Real Kite Day, Plaza Camino Real Shopping Mall, Carlsbad, CA. *Sponsor and contact*: Plaza Camino Real, Carlsbad, CA 92008. 3rd annual in 1978.

Second March Saturday: Ocean Beach Kite Festival and Parade, San Diego, CA. *Sponsors*: San Diego Park and Recreation Department, Ocean Beach Recreation Council and Kiwanis Club. *Contact*: Don Hodo, 4726 Santa Monica Avenue, San Diego, CA 92107. 30th annual in 1978.

Late March Saturday: Ben Franklin Kite Day, San Francisco, CA. *Sponsor*: San Francisco Recreation and Park Department. *Contact*: Ron Juvland, McLaren Lodge, Golden Gate Park, San Francisco, CA 94117. 3rd annual in 1978.

Fourth Saturdays in March, July, and October: Venice Pier Kite Festival, Venice, CA. Also Mini-Festivals 4th Saturdays every month. *Sponsor and contact*: Let's Fly a Kite (c/o Gloria Lugo), Fisherman's Village, 13763 Fiji Way, Marina del Rey, CA 90291. 5th annual series in 1978.

Second April Saturday: Carmel Kite Festival, Carmel, CA. *Sponsors*: Carmel Unified School District and Carmel Lions Club. *Contact*: Pat Cunningham, Recreation Department, Carmel Unified School District, Drawer U–1, Carmel, CA 93921. 48th annual in 1978.

Second April Sunday: Sunshine Kite Festival, Redondo Beach, CA. *Sponsor and contact*: Sunshine Kite Company (c/o Randy Joe), 223–B Fisherman's Wharf, Redondo Beach, CA 90277. 3rd annual in 1978.

Third April Saturday: Long Beach International Kite Festival, Long Beach, CA. Also International Kite Fight the day after. *Sponsor and contact*: Long Beach Recreation Department (c/o Maria Sharpe), 155 Queens Way Landing, Long Beach, CA 90803. 52nd annual in 1978.

Father's Day, Third June Sunday: Father's Day Kite Festival, San Francisco, CA. Also, in preceding week, Indoor Kiteflying Competition. *Sponsors*: Anchor Steam Beer, KFRC Radio and Come Fly a Kite, Inc. *Contact*: Ron Young of Solutions, 507 Howard Street, San Francisco, CA 94105. 6th annual in 1978.

Second August Saturday: Kite-Nic, Mission Bay, San Diego, CA. *Sponsor and contact*: San Diego Kite Club (c/o Vic Heredia), P. O. Box 3248, San Diego, CA 92103. 3rd annual in 1978.

## Delaware

Good Friday: Great Delaware Kite Festival, Lewes, DE. *Sponsor and contact*: Lewes Chamber of Commerce, P. O. Box 1, Lewes, DE 19958. 7th annual in 1978.

## District of Columbia

Last March Saturday: Smithsonian Kite Carnival, Washington, D.C. *Sponsors*: Smithsonian Resident Associates, National Capital Parks Commission and DC Recreation Department. *Contact*: Smithsonian Resident Associates (c/o Tina Parker), Smithsonian Institution, Washington, D.C. 20560. 12th annual in 1978.

## Florida

Third January Saturday: International Kite Flying Contest, Sarasota, FL. *Sponsor and contact*: Sheraton Sandcastle Resort (c/o V. Ward Bennett), 1540 Benjamin Franklin Drive, Sarasota, FL 33577. 10th annual in 1978.

Last February Saturday: Kite Festival, Orlando, FL. *Sponsor and contact*: Associate Board of Loch Haven Arts Center (c/o Kite Festival Chairman), 2416 N. Mills Avenue, Orlando, FL 32803. 3rd annual in 1978.

Last February weekend: Jacksonville Kite Contest, Jacksonville, FL. *Sponsor and contact*: Jacksonville Department of Recreation and Public Affairs (c/o Gary Kirkland), 851 N. Market Street, Jacksonville, FL 32202. 53rd annual in 1978.

## Georgia

First April Saturday: Endurance Kite Flying Contest, Stone Mountain, GA. *Sponsor and contact*: Stone Mountain Park (c/o Betsy Sheehan), P. O. Box 778, Stone Mountain, GA 30086. 8th annual in 1978.

## Hawaii

Third March Saturday: Oahu Kite Flying Contest, Oahu, HI. *Sponsors*: Honolulu Department of Parks and Recreation, KJMB TV and Radio, and Hawaiian Electric Company. *Contact*: Don Fujii, Sport Section, 650 S. King Street, Honolulu, HI 96813. 11th annual in 1978.

## Idaho

Late April Saturday: Freeman Park Fly-In, Idaho Falls, ID. *Sponsor*: Bonneville-Idaho Falls Parks and Recreation Department (c/o John Johnson), Box 220, Idaho Falls, ID 83401. 5th annual in 1978.

## Illinois

Early April weekend: Amelia Earhart Memorial Kite Fly, Illinois Institute of Technology, Chicago, IL. *Sponsors*: Radio WOUI and Illinois Institute of Technology. *Contact*: Rich Unger, 3241 S. Federal, Chicago, IL 60616.

Last April Sunday: "I Love You Chicago" Kite Fly, Chicago, IL. *Sponsors*: WIND Radio and Chicago Park District. *Contact*: WIND Radio (c/o Jill O'Mahony), 625 N. Michigan Avenue, Chicago, IL 60611. 12th annual in 1978.

## Iowa

Fourth April Saturday: Kiwanis Kite Tournament, Sac City, IA. *Sponsor and contact*: Sac City Kiwanis Club (c/o Gary Hansen), 508 S. 13th Street, Sac City, IA 50583. 53rd annual in 1978.

## Louisiana

Third March Sunday: New Orleans Kite Festival, New Orleans, LA. *Sponsors*: The Kite Shop—Jackson Square, and WRNO Radio. *Contact*: The Kite Shop—Jackson Square (c/o Sally Fontana), 542 St. Peter Street, New Orleans, LA 70116. 6th annual in 1978.

## Maryland

First April Saturday: Ben Franklin Kite Contest, Takoma Park, MD. *Sponsor and contact*: Takoma Park Recreation Department and Council (c/o Belle Ziegler), 7500 Maple Avenue, Takoma Park, MD 20012.

Last April Saturday: Maryland Kite Festival, Baltimore, MD. *Sponsor and contact*: Maryland Kite Society, P. O. Box 10467, Baltimore, MD 21209. 12th annual in 1978.

Mid-August Sunday: Sunny Sunday Kite Fly, Baltimore, MD. *Sponsor*: Downtown Coordinating Committee: *Contact*: Maryland Kite Society, P. O. Box 10467, Baltimore, MD 21209. 5th annual in 1978.

Last October Sunday: Windsor Hills Fall Kite Fly, Baltimore, MD. *Sponsor*: Windsor Hills Neighbors, Inc. *Contact*: Maryland Kite Society, P. O. Box 10467, Baltimore, MD 21209. 6th annual in 1978.

## Massachusetts

Second May Saturday: Great Boston Kite Festival, Boston, MA. *Sponsor and contact*: Committee for the Better Use of Air (c/o Gill Fishman), 23 Arrow Street, Cambridge, MA 02138. 10th annual in 1978.

Third August Saturday: Cape Cod Kite Festival, Provincetown, MA. *Sponsor and contact*: Outermost Kites (c/o Gabriel Dix), P. O. Box 1032, Provincetown, Cape Cod, MA 02657. 4th annual in 1978.

## New Jersey

Fourth of July: Kite Flying Festival, Ocean City, NJ. *Sponsor*: Ocean City Recreation Department. *Contact*: Ocean City Public Relations Department (c/o Mark Soifer), P. O. Box 174, Ocean City, NJ 08226.

## New York

Early October Sunday: New York City Kite Festival, Central Park, New York, NY. *Sponsor and contact*: Go Fly a Kite, Inc., 1434 Third Avenue, New York, NY 10028. 4th annual in 1978.

## North Carolina

First April Saturday: Great Outta Sight Kite Flight, Charlotte, NC. *Sponsor and contact*: Charlotte Recreation Department (c/o Joyce Hoyle), P. O. Box 4008, Charlotte, NC 28204. 13th annual in 1978.

Third July Saturday: Galleon Esplanade Kite Contest, Nags Head, NC. *Sponsor and contact*: Galleon Esplanade (c/o Kay Culpepper), P. O. Box 67, Nags Head, NC 27959. 7th annual in 1978.

## Ohio
April through September monthly flies: *Sponsor and contact*: Ohio Society for the Elevation of Kites (c/o Thomas Rask, President), 2687 E. 128 Street, Cleveland, OH 44120.

Third May Sunday: Kite Day, Stow, OH. *Sponsor and contact*: Stow Parks and Recreation Department (c/o Al Weiler), 3760 Darrow Road, Stow, OH 44224. 4th annual in 1978.

Second August Saturday: Cleveland Games Kite-In, Cleveland, OH. *Sponsor and contact*: Ohio Society for the Elevation of Kites (c/o Thomas Rask), 2687 E. 128th Street, Cleveland, OH 44120.

## Oklahoma
Third March Sunday: Kite Flite, Tulsa, OK. *Sponsors*: River Parks Authority, Tulsa Park and Recreation Department, and KMOD/KXXO Radio. *Contact*: River Parks Authority (c/o Vivian Steele-Shellshear), 411 S. Denver, Tulsa, OK 74103. 3rd annual in 1978.

## South Carolina
First April Saturday: Kite Contest, Charleston, SC (site revolves from Charleston to Florence to Columbia). *Sponsor and contact*: Florence Kite Flying Association (c/o Robert F. Liger, Jr.), 1807 Hazel Drive, Florence, SC 29501. 6th annual in 1978.

## Tennessee
Mid-April Saturday: Nashville Kite Flite, Nashville, TN. *Sponsors*: Horizons, Ltd., and Metro Nashville Park Board. *Contact*: Horizons, Ltd. (c/o Natalie May), 2224 Bandywood, Nashville, TN 37215. 4th annual in 1978.

## Texas
Mid-March Saturday: Kite Fair, San Antonio, TX. *Sponsors*: KITE Radio and San Antonio Department of Parks and Recreation. *Contact*: Department of Parks and Recreation (c/o Phyllis Alvarez), 950 E. Hildebrand, San Antonio, TX 78212. 18th annual in 1978.

Mid-March Sunday: Zilker Park Kite Tournament, Austin, TX. *Sponsors*: Austin Exchange Club, Austin Parks and Recreation Department and Radio KOKE.

*Contact*: Richard S. Robertson, 5401 Shoalwood Avenue, Austin, TX 78756. 50th annual in 1978.

## Vermont
First May Sunday: Essex Junction Kite Contest, Essex Center, VT. *Sponsors*: Gil Myers and Frank Roeber. *Contact*: Art Stultz, 37 Birchwood Drive, Colchester, VT 05446. 5th annual in 1978.

## Virginia
Third March Saturday: Gunston Hall Kite Festival, Lorton, VA. *Sponsor and contact*: Gunston Hall Plantation (c/o Louise Stockdale), Lorton, VA 22079. 7th annual in 1978.

## Washington
Mid-July Saturday: Port of Seattle/Seafair Kite Contest. *Contact*: Washington Kitefliers Association, c/o Pacific Science Center, 200 Second Avenue N., Seattle, WA 98109. 3rd annual in 1978.

Late July Saturday: Seafair/Capital Hill Chamber of Commerce Kite Festival, Seattle, WA. *Contact*: Washington Kitefliers Association, c/o Pacific Science Center, 200 Second Avenue N., Seattle, WA 98109. 6th annual in 1978.

## West Virginia
June or July Sunday: Harpers Ferry Family Fly, Harpers Ferry, WV. *Contact*: Maryland Kite Society, P. O. Box 10467, Baltimore, MD 21209. 7th annual in 1978.

## Wisconsin
First May Sunday: WIBA-FM Kite Fly-In, Madison, WI. *Sponsor and contact*: WIBA-FM Radio (c/o Mini Murphy), P. O. Box 99, Madison, WI 53701. 4th annual in 1978.

## Canada
Second April Sunday: Great Pacific Rim Kite Festival, Vancouver, British Columbia. *Sponsor and contact*: High as a Kite (c/o Marcia Madill), No. 201, 131 Water Street, Vancouver, British Columbia V6B 4M3. 3rd annual in 1978.

Third July Sunday: St. John's Kite Festival, St. Johns, Newfoundland. *Sponsor and contact*: Memorial University Extension Service, 21 King's Bridge Road, St. Johns, Newfoundland. 7th annual in 1978.

Last August Sunday: Canadian National Exhibition Kite Festival, Toronto, Ontario. *Sponsor and contact*: Canadian National Exhibition (c/o Sports Department), Exhibition Place, Toronto, Ontario M6K 3C3.

# Kite Associations

American Kitefliers Association
7106 Campfield Road
Baltimore, MD 21207
(Publishes a quarterly journal, *Kite Lines*; $6 per
    year)

## Chapters of AKA

### California
San Diego Kite Club
c/o R. Victor Heredia
P. O. Box 3248
San Diego, CA 92103

### Colorado
Beulah Valley Association for Tethered Flight
c/o Frances Weaver
8969 Squirrel Creek Road
Beulah, CO 81023

### Delaware
Delaware Kite Club
c/o Dr. Floyd Cornelison, Jr., President
16 Stonehill Road
Wilmington, DE 19803

### Hawaii
Hawaii Chapter, AKA
c/o Wayne Baldwin, President
47–120 Uakoko Place
Kaneohe, HI 96744

### Maryland
Maryland Kite Society
c/o Theodore L. Manekin, Executive Secretary
8 Charles Plaza #1807
Baltimore, MD 21201

### New York
Long Meadow Chapter, AKA
c/o Edwin L. Grauel
799 Elmwood Terrace
Rochester, NY 14620

Utica Chapter, AKA
c/o Betty Devins
1038 Albany Street
Utica, NY 13501

### Ohio
Ohio Society for the Elevation of Kites
c/o Thomas Rask, President
2687 East 128 Street
Cleveland, OH 44120

### South Carolina
Florence Kite Flying Association
c/o Robert F. Liger, Jr.
1807 Hazel Drive
Florence, SC 29501

### Washington
Washington Kitefliers Association
c/o The Pacific Science Center
200 Second Avenue North
Seattle, WA 98109

### Foreign
Australian Kite Association
c/o Helen Bushell, Secretary
10 Elm Grove, North Kew 3102
Victoria, Australia

Waikato Chapter, AKA
c/o Logan Fow, Secretary-Treasurer
62 Paul Crescent
Hamilton, New Zealand

## Unaffiliated Associations

### Australia
Kite Fliers Association of South Australia
c/o Ian Perrin, Secretary-Treasurer
69 Fisher Street
Myrtle Bank, South Australia 5064

### France
Le Cerf-Volant Club de France
c/o Jean-Louis Bouisset, President
17 rue Lacharrière
75011 Paris

### Great Britain
British Kite Flying Association
c/o Ron Moulton
P. O. Box 35 Bridge Street
Hemel, Hempstead, Herts. HP1 1EE

Essex Kite Group
c/o Clive C. O. Rawlinson
The Croft, Howe Street
Gt. Waltham, Chelmsford, Essex

European Kitefliers Association
c/o Nick Laurie
Longstone Lodge, Aller
Langport, Somerset
(Publishes a quarterly magazine, *European Kiteflier*)

Japan
Create Kitefliers Club, Japan
Matsuo Isobe, Managing Director
c/o Noritsu Machinery Manufacturing Co., Ltd.
14–13, 5–Chome, Ebara
Shinagawa-Ku, Tokyo

Japan Kite Association
c/o Shingo Modegi, President
c/o Taimeiken
1 Chome, 12–10 Nihonbashi
Chuoku, Tokyo

Malta
Malta Kitefliers Group
c/o A. Darmenia-Gay, Secretary
2, Princess Anne Flats, Ball Street
Paceville, Malta GC

United States
Connecticut Kitefliers Association
c/o Doug Allen
4–L Lakeside Drive
Ledyard, CT 06339

The Marina Greeners
c/o Brendan Michael Cooke
8712 Sturgeon Way
Sacramento, CA 95826

Marine Park Kite Fliers Association
c/o Joe Manzi, Jr.
20 Colin Place
Brooklyn, NY 11223

# Kite Specialty Shops

The following is a selected list of kite shops in the United States and Canada. At this writing, approximately one hundred such shops are doing business in this speciality, which was pioneered by Go Fly a Kite, Inc., in New York City. Their first tiny store opened for business in May 1965. Especially in the last four years, kite shops have proliferated in response to the growing interest in kites and the variety of fine models available. The shops are often whimsically named; it seems one of the first challenges for a new shop is to come up with a clever moniker that no one else has used before.

Kite shops today vary in more than their names. Some have only a limited stock of kites; others carry practically every kite manufactured. The better stores will have at least a well-chosen, representative selection in a wide price range. Many shops cater to the complete kiteflier by carrying line, reels, accessories, kite-making materials, and kite books and magazines. Also, a good kite shop can be judged by the steadiness of its services. Except in resort areas, it should be open year-round, even if the hours are reduced in the colder months. Finally, you will know a good kite shop by its professionalism—admittedly a quality that is difficult to define. Does this shop give service, repair kites, advise you about flying different models, encourage and inform you? Is the display attractive, the atmosphere personal?

The ideal kite emporium may be as elusive as the ideal kite, but the following list includes shops that seem to be true kite shops (that is, devoted especially to kites), complete, professional, and (except as noted) open year-round.

No claim is made for the completeness of this list, which is subject to time's inevitable changes.

**Alaska**
Whittlewinds Gallery
Country Village Mall
700 E. Benson Boulevard
Anchorage, AK 99503

**Arizona**
The Kite Shop
A & M Pump & Pool Supply
1313 S. Country Club Drive
Mesa, AZ 95202

**California**
Above & Beyond
1510–G Walnut Square
Berkeley, CA 94709

Come Fly a Kite, Inc.
Carmel Plaza
Carmel, CA 93921

Come Fly a Kite, Inc.
Ghirardelli Square
900 North Point
San Francisco, CA 94109

Fly a Kite
South Coast Village
3850 S. Plaza Drive
Santa Ana, CA 92707

High as a Kite
691 Bridgeway
Sausalito, CA 94965

Kite & Gift
Fisherman's Wharf
333 Jefferson Street, No. 7
San Francisco, CA 94133

Kite City
1201 Front Street
Old Sacramento, CA 95814

The Kite Store
973 Grand Avenue
Pacific Beach, CA 92109

Kites & Strings
740 Ventura Place
San Diego, CA 92109

Kites Kites Kites
Jakopane—Jack London Village
55 Alice Street
Oakland, CA 94607

Krazy Kites
778 Higuera Street, #3
San Luis Obispo, CA 93401

Let's Fly a Kite
Fisherman's Village
13763 Fiji Way
Marina del Rey, CA 90291

The Red Balloon Kite Shop
In the Vineyard, 1523 E.
Valley Parkway
Escondido, CA 92027

Sunshine Kite Company
233-B Fisherman's Wharf
Redondo Beach Pier
Redondo Beach, CA 90277

You've Got Me Flying
123 Pearl Alley
Santa Cruz, CA 95060

Colorado
The Kite Store in Larimer Square
1430 Larimer Street
Denver, CO 80202

Skyscrapers Kites
2563 Fifteenth Street
Denver, CO 80211

Connecticut
The Ben Franklin Kite Shoppe
One-Half Pearl Street
Mystic, CT 06355

District of Columbia
The Kite Site
1075 Wisconsin Avenue, N.W.
Georgetown, DC 20007

Florida
Come Fly a Kite
313 Clearwater Mall
International Bazaar, 2nd level
Clearwater, FL 33518

Heavenly Body Kites
409 Greene Street
Key West, FL 33040

The Kite Shop
1642 W. University Avenue
Gainesville, FL 32601

Hawaii
Starships & Strings
75-5699-D Alii Drive
Kailua-Kona, HI 96740

Illinois
Windy City Kite Works, Ltd.
2828 N. Clark Street
Chicago, IL 60657

Louisiana
The Kite Shop—Jackson Square
542 St. Peter Street
New Orleans, LA 70116

Kites of All Nations
603 Royal Street
New Orleans, LA 70130

Maryland
The Kite Loft (seasonal)
5 N. Second Street
Ocean City, MD 21842

Kites Aweigh
36 Market Street
Annapolis, MD 21401

Massachusetts
Outermost Kites (seasonal)
Union Square
Provincetown, Cape Cod, MA 02657

Michigan
The Unique Place—World of Kites
344 Hamilton Row
Birmingham, MI 48011

Missouri
Augusta Wind Kites (seasonal)
Country Club Plaza
Kansas City, MO 64112

Riverwind Kite Works (seasonal)
612 N. Second Street
Lacledes Landing
St. Louis, MO 63102

New York
Go Fly a Kite, Inc.
1434 Third Avenue
New York, NY 10028

Go Fly a Kite, Inc.
79 Job's Lane
Southampton, NY 11968

Ohio
The Kite Kompany, Inc.
33 West Orange
Chagrin Falls, OH 44022

Oregon
Kites and Other Delights
99 W. 10th Street, Suite 120
Eugene, OR 97401

Once Upon a Breeze
253 N. Hemlock
Cannon Beach, OR 97110

Wind Play
212 N. W. Couch
Portland, OR 97209

Pennsylvania
Windfall, Inc.
New Market Square
2nd and Pine Streets
Philadelphia, PA 19147

Washington
Great Winds
Pioneer Square
166 S. Jackson Street
Seattle, WA 98104

Wisconsin
Fish Creek Kite Company
R. R. 1, Box 205—Highway 42
Fish Creek, WI 54212

The Kite Farm
728 University Avenue
Madison, WI 53715

Canada
Le Cerf-Volant (seasonal)
1393 E. Dorchester
Montreal, Quebec

High as a Kite
201-131 Water Street
Vancouver, B. C., Canada V6B 4M3

The Kite Store
848-A Yonge Street
Toronto, Ontario, Canada M4W 2H1

# Bibliography

## English-Language References

Bahadur of India. *India Fighter Kites*. Go Fly a Kite, 1434 Third Avenue, New York, N.Y. 10028, 1960. This eight-page pamphlet provides useful information on Indian fighter kites.

Brummitt, Wyatt. *Kites*. New York: Golden Press, Western Publishing Co., Inc., 1971. Most of what there is to know about kites in digest form.

Downer, Marion. *Kites: How to Make and Fly Them*. New York: Lothrop, 1959. An introduction to kites with easy-to-use photos and illustrations.

Fowler, H. Waller. *Kites: A Practical Guide to Kite Making and Flying*. 4th ed. New York: Ronald, 1965. An illustrated guide to kite fundamentals, including reels and other equipment, for young readers.

Greger, Margaret. *Blown Sky-High*. Richland, Washington, 1977. Proven kite-making methods for children and adults working with them.

Hart, Clive. *Kites: An Historical Survey*. New York: Frederick A. Praeger, 1967. An anthropological history of kites, now out of print.

———. *The Dream of Flight*. New York: Winchester Press, 1972. A documented account of the renaissance of aeronautics in the classical period.

———. *Your Book of Kites*. New York: Transatlantic Art, Inc., 1964. A creative approach to kite-making for young readers.

Hunt, Leslie L. *Getting Started in Kitemaking*. The Bruce Publishing Co., 1929, 1971. A guide for constructing representative American kites, with color photos and working diagrams. Now out of print.

———. *Twenty-five Kites That Fly*. New York: Dover Publications, 1971. A re-publication of the 1929 edition with its panoply of twenty-five types of kites.

Jue, David. *Chinese Kites*. Rutland, Vermont: Tuttle, 1967. A well-made book about well-made kites in the Chinese tradition.

Kettlekamp, Larry. *Kites*. New York: William Morrow, 1959. A well-put-together 48-page book for youngsters.

*Kite Lines*, the quarterly journal of the American Kiteflyers Association, published by Verve Enterprises, Inc., 7106 Campbell Road, Baltimore, Maryland 21207.

Mouvier, Jean-Paul. *Kites!* New York: Watts, 1974. Compact pocketbook, fresh, fanciful, and colorful.

Neal, Harry E. *The Story of the Kite*. New York: Vanguard Press, 1954. Well-written illustrated history of kites for the younger set.

Newman, Lee and Jay. *Kite Craft*. New York: Crown Publishers, Inc., 1974. A well-illustrated guide to kite history and kite-making.

Pelham, David. *The Penguin Book of Kites*. New York: Penguin Books, 1976. Most comprehensive collection of kite plans yet available.

Saito, Tadao. *High Fliers*. Tokyo: Japan Publications, 1969. An English introduction to representative Japanese kites by Tadao Saito of the Japan Kite Association.

Streeter, Tal. *The Art of the Japanese Kite*. New York and Tokyo: Weatherhill, 1974. Essayistic accounts of the sculptor-author's meetings with Japanese kite-makers; fine photographs.

Wagenvoord, James. *Flying Kites*. New York: Macmillan, 1969. Many photos of kiting as a sport. Includes building instructions.

Yolen, Jane. *World on a String: The Story of Kites*. New York: Collins-World, 1975. An approach to kite history through research data and contemporary photos.

Yolen, Will. *The Complete Book of Kites and Kite Flying*. New York: Simon & Schuster, 1976. A kite-flying storybook.

## Japanese-Language References

Hiroi, Tsutomu. *Tako* (Kites). Bijutsu Shuppansha, 1969.

———. *Tako* (Kites). Mainichi Shimbunsha, 1973.

———. *Rittai-dako* (Three-dimensional Kites). Tokuma Shoten, 1975.

———. *Tezukuri no tako* (Handmade Kites). Rippu Shobo, 1975.

———. *Tezukuri sekai no tako* (Illustrated World Kite Making). Rippu Shobo, 1976.

Inoue, Shigeyoshi. *Nihon no tako* (Japanese Kites). Akashimame Honranbu Yosho, 1972.

Kuroda, Ryuji. *Rittai-dako* (Three-dimensional Kites). Seibundo Shinkosha, 1975.

Miyama. Goro. *Tako no hon* (A Book of Kites). Shinshindo Shuppan, 1975.

Motoyama, Keisen. *Nihon minzoku zushi* (Japanese Folklore Illustrated). Tokyodo, 1942.

Niizaka, Kazuo. *Hatsumei-dako* (Invention Kites). Fukuinkan Shoten, 1975.

Nishibayashi, Takeshi. *Sosaku no tako* (Creative Kites). Tokuma Shoten, 1973.

Nishimoto, Morisaka. *Okinawa no tako* (Okinawan Kites). Hirugi-sha, 1975.

Noguchi, Tesutaro. *Origami tako* (Origami Kites). Tokuma Shoten, 1976.

Saito, Tadao. *Tako no katachi* (Kite Form). Iwasaki Bijutsusha, 1971.

———. *Tako-zukuri* (Kite-making). Hoikusha, 1975.

———. Ichiro Hike, and Shingo Modegi. *Tako*: *tsukurikata agekata* (Kites: Making and Flying Them). Tokuma Shoten, 1973.

———. Shingo Modegi, Tsutomu Hiroi, Ichiro Hike. *Nihon no tako daizenshu*. Tokuma Shoten, 1976.

Tawara, Yusaku, ed. *Nihon no tako* (Japanese Kites). Bijutsu Shuppansha, 1964.

———. *Nihon no tako* (Japanese Kites). Kikukasha, 1969.

Watanabe, Moriwaka, ed. *Yokaichi odako chosa hokoku-sho* (Yokaichi Giant Kite Survey Report). 1969.